LIVING AND WORKING WITH
THE HORSE OF SPAIN

LIVING AND WORKING
WITH THE
HORSE OF SPAIN

Peter Maddison-Greenwell and Jane Lake

J.A. ALLEN · LONDON

© Peter Maddison-Greenwell and Jane Lake
First published in Great Britain 2006

ISBN-10: 0 85131 885 1
ISBN-13: 978 0 85131 885 1

J. A. Allen
Clerkenwell House
Clerkenwell Green
London EC1R OHT

J. A. Allen is an imprint of Robert Hale Limited

The right of Peter Maddison-Greenwell and Jane Lake to be identified
as authors of this work has been asserted by them in accordance
with the Copyright, Designs and Patents Act 1988

A catalogue record for this book is available from the British Library

Photographs by, or property of, the authors, except for those on page xviii (Campbell Young);
page xxii (Brooke Cramton); page 21 (Kathy Graves); page 25 (Martha Holly); page 41 (top right)
(Bob Langrish); Page 95 (Courtesy Sylvia Loch), Page 122 (Elizabeth Furth), pages 4 and 5 (Frank
Mansell); pages 99–101, 103–4 (Hon. Lucinda Wynn); pages xvii, 39 (bottom), 131, 184 (Phillip
Stewart); pages 77, 79, 83, 84 (courtesy Ludomar); pages 46, 48, 49, 53, 58, 148 (Rafael Lemos);
pages 6, 7, 8, 26, 36, 67, 80, 88, 89, 91, 93 (Florence Hunt); pages xix, 12, 29, 30, 32, 33 (bottom),
39 (top), 56, 127, 144, 145, 162, 178 (Jenny Goodhall).

Edited by Martin Diggle
Design and typesetting by Paul Saunders

Colour separation by Tenon & Polert Colour Scanning Limited, Hong Kong
Printed by New Era Printing Co. Limited, Hong Kong

To my closest friends and family, without whom life would be neither possible nor worthwhile, and to my horses, who have given me their liberty without either choice or complaint.

PETER MADDISON-GREENWELL

Contents

Acknowledgements

Having worked mainly on separate parts of the book, we have different people to thank but we are both extremely grateful for all the help, encouragement and support we have received from all quarters.

First, I must thank Danielle Lawniczak, my partner, without whom none of this would have been possible. She has supported me in all I do and has allowed me to fulfil my dreams and shared in so many of them; thank you, it has been a gift few others would give so generously.

To my family, who have always supported me both as a child and an adult, I wish you were all here now so that I could say I love you and thank you.

Thank you to the El Caballo de España team and my other treasured true friends, who are always there when I need them and never there when I do not. You have been my sanity and my survival.

To ex-policeman Eric Read who treated me like a son and taught me to ride a horse and drive a car (both on occasions 'with great speed'), thank you for being such a great inspiration and for living so long, which enabled me to learn so much from you in so many ways.

I am also grateful to ex-cavalry officer Bob Holmes with whom I spent so much time as a teenager riding Lord Rothschild's polo ponies and hunters. Bob's precision cleaning and pristine presentation will stay with me for ever. He virtually gave me an army training without my having to leave home. Thank you Bob.

To Juan Llamas whom I met many years ago when I first started working with Spanish horses. He has been a great inspiration as an author, an artist, a poet and most certainly a leading authority on the Spanish horse. His book *This is the Spanish Horse* has been a constant source of reference.

I also wish to say a special thank you to my new-found American friends,

Brooke and Kathy and the growing number of people who have given me their time and support and who have opened their homes and hearts to me.

Thank you too, to the Honourable Lucinda Wynn and Florence Hunt, for their photographs. Good photographs are an essential part of a book of this type, and there are two professional photographers I would also like to thank for their wonderful art.

Rafael Lemos was born in Los Palacios y Villafranca, next to the *marismas* (marshes) of the Guadalquivir River in Seville, Andalusia. A professional photographer through family tradition, and equine photographer owing to his interest in, and love for, horses, Rafael's work represents the era of maximum splendour of the equestrian world in Andalusia and throughout Spain. His work captures magical moments and is a testimony to the equestrian evolution of Andalusian horses during the last quarter century: *doma vaquera*, driving, dressage, *acoso y derribo* and the conformation shows. Rafael's artistic career has been recognized both in Europe and in America.

Jenny Goodhall is a well-known photographer and winner of many awards and prizes for her art. I owe her special thanks for all her support and for capturing some of our most precious moments on film.

PETER MADDISON-GREENWELL

I AM MOST GRATEFUL to the Harry Ransom Humanities Research Center, The University of Texas at Austin, for permission to print the extracts from *Centaurs of Many Lands* by Edward Larocque Tinker, and to my Texan cousin, Susan Roe Jernigan, who made the initial contact with the extremely helpful Margaret Tenney at the Research Center on my behalf.

I am also very grateful to Jan Morris for her permission to print extracts from her wonderful book *Spain*, and Alex Holroyd at Random House, London, for her assistance in this matter.

My thanks also go to Sylvia Loch for supplying the photograph on page 95, to Elizabeth Furth for permission to use her photograph on page 122, and to Frank Mansell for his permission to use his photographs in The Andalusian Ethos chapter.

Thank you to Caroline Burt, former publisher at J. A. Allen, for her belief in this project and my love for the subject, to Cassie Campbell, commissioning editor at J. A. Allen, for her patience, to Martin Diggle whose thoughtful and constructive editorial tweaks and suggestions have smoothed the book's path, and to Paul Saunders whose design skills add so much to the finished product.

To Dave Charnley, a true horseman, with whom I share so much, my love and thanks.

I also thank Carol Robertson, a very special friend, for, amongst so many other things, her patient help every time I'm ready to throw the computer out of the window.

Finally, my love and thanks to my mother who, like all mothers, believes her child's talent is far greater than it really is.

JANE LAKE

Prefaces

HAVING TAKEN EVERY opportunity to ride since the age of nine, I must by now have spent thousands of hours in the company of horses. Since childhood I have ridden nearly every kind of horse from jumpers, racehorses, hunters and polo ponies, to show horses, dressage horses and, most latterly, Spanish horses.

My introduction to the Spanish horse came with a horse called Chico (a Hispano Arabe) who was to inspire my partner Danielle and me to take on the biggest challenge of our lives. Chico was bought from Jenny Bernard, his breeder, who was then secretary and registrar of The British Andalusian Horse Society, which is now The British Association for the Pure-bred Spanish Horse. There were not many members and there were even fewer Spanish horses registered in Great Britain at that time. It was Jenny's kindness and encouragement that led me to get completely involved with the society, and within a short time I was on the committee. I soon realized that 'committee' meant 'committed' – and you had to be.

Danielle and I were hooked, however, and we took Chico to every event we could. In his first two years of schooling, this wonderful horse won all the society's prizes and awards in the ridden classes, even when competing against Pure-bred stallions. He became an ambassador for the society and the greatest teacher one could ask for. It was this kind, patient, talented horse who allowed us to learn *doma vaquera* (the stockman's dressage), work with the *garrocha* (the stockman's bull-controlling pole), *trabajo a la mano* (work in-hand), and the use of the *reindas largos* (long-reins) as well as letting me experiment with all the training techniques I had learnt from books, clinics, videos and other trainers.

Finally, after many years of loyal service, I had to make the decision to retire Chico from serious work at the age of twenty-one because he was gradually losing his sight. We retired him in 2001 at the breed association annual gala. This was a most moving occasion, with his last *garrocha* performance being encapsulated between two piercing spotlights projecting a twenty-foot silhouette of us both on the wall. At the end he stood absolutely still, noble and alert in a single beam of light, with not even a flicker of an ear as I removed his saddle and laid it gently in the other light beam. We were then joined by Jenny who led him for his last parade. The audience were both elated and moved to tears; many of them had watched him grow up and develop and supported him over the previous sixteen years, and had become our friends.

From this humble beginning with just one part-bred Spanish horse, my insatiable thirst for knowledge of all things connected with these fascinating horses grew and started the journey that has made my life complete. It has been the catalyst for some of the most loyal and honest friendships one could wish for and it has awakened a depth of emotion that makes one realize what makes living so special.

The ever-giving character of the Spanish horse allows us to share his strength, stamina and beauty of movement (despite our sometimes ignorant and flawed ideals) and, once in a while, if we are very fortunate, also to share a fleeting moment of true harmony with another being.

However we choose to work with the Spanish horse, it is imperative that his wonderful character is retained. We should present him with the integrity his history commands, for surely he has earned his reputation as the Legend of Spain.

El Caballo de España

'El Caballo de España' is the name by which I, together with Danielle and a group of close friends, have promoted Spanish and Lusitano horses since 1988. We have dedicated much of our lives to this promotion and it is with some pride, and much gratitude, that I relate how this passion has filled our lives and given us so much.

Since, in 1988, there were only a few Spanish and Lusitano pure-bred and part-bred horses in the UK, we decided to present the Iberian horse to the

British public in a way that we hoped would ensure that he would be appreciated both for his history and in the modern equestrian world.

Initially we gave our displays at small events such as church fêtes and bar mitzvahs, but we rapidly became an equestrian display team that was topping the bill at some of the most prestigious venues and events in the UK. We had soon performed for a number of well-known companies including Iberia Airlines, San Miguel, Seat Cars and Compaq computers.

Within eight years of the formation of El Caballo de España, we had learnt a great deal and soon progressed from the early shows, which were simply scaled-down versions of the displays of the Royal School in Jerez, to shows with a creative and varied content which were completely different from any other display. We brought the art of the *garrochista* to the British audiences and performed the movements of passage, piaffe, Spanish walk, reversed pirouettes on three legs (in which the horse pivots on one foreleg with the

Peter Maddison-Greenwell riding the Spanish Stallion, Farolero, at a Viva España show at Olympia.

Some of the El Caballo de España display team stabled at the Royal Mews.

other held out as in Spanish walk), levade and pesade, doing these in a balletic way: interpreting inspirational music into movement. We have also incorporated flamenco guitarists and dancers into the performances, and even used fire to create a theatrical effect.

In 1996 I produced a show entitled 'The Legend of Spain' and had begun to market the team as an 'Equestrian Theatre – the first in England'. We were beginning to push out the boundaries of equestrian art. The first showing of 'The Legend of Spain' was at the Roundhouse in Camden and, because we were given very little time before opening night, I had to design the posters, do the radio interviews, produce the show – and I even came up with some of the ideas for the lighting effects. Once I had also choreographed the show, selected the poems, written the narration and chosen the music, all that was left to do was to sell out and perform. This we did, and to great reviews.

This confirmed that the format was sound, and so we recreated ourselves as 'The First Equestrian Theatre'. Since that time we have produced a new 'Legend of Spain' each year. We also devise other shows with different themes and ideas.

Danielle Lawniczak on Saeta performing the reversed pirouette on three legs. The first two photographs show the hind legs crossing over as the horse pirouettes around the forehand. Note the foreleg held up in the fashion of the Spanish walk – the art lies in moving fluently from the Spanish walk into the reversed pirouette, and returning to it with equal fluency afterwards. The Spanish walk itself is shown in the final photograph.

We shall continue to present the horse of Spain to the British public and know that his unique beauty and qualities will endear him to an ever-wider audience.

Our sensitive Spanish and Lusitano stallions are also used to inspire people in a far less public way. With our dear friend and partner Dr Alison Winch we devised a developmental course for individuals and companies in which our horses show people how to develop their confidence and self-esteem in a way that can be life changing.

When we started this work, Alison was the Human Resources director for a large, well-known company in the brewing industry. I remember the day she arrived in our drive, got out of her car and, with the biggest, warmest of Irish smiles, said: 'I saw you perform last night – I want to work with you'.

We became great friends and I learnt so much from her, as did all the team. She showed us how to look more closely at ourselves, our feelings and emotions, and the ways in which we learnt and taught.

She told me that what I do naturally with both the horses and human pupils, and the way in which we worked as a team, was exactly what she wanted to promote with her courses for 'organizational and personal development'. Those things we look for in our relationships with our horses are metaphors for everything we require in all our relationships throughout life: harmony, communication, inspiration, energy, passion and all the other important factors.

After two years working together on this inspirational and successful project, Alison took us into her confidence and told us she had been diagnosed with cancer. We watched helplessly as this remarkable lady took on this, the greatest test of courage, with dignity and selflessness. She passed on early in 2005, leaving behind many grateful people who were the better for knowing her.

Alison's husband Steve, whom I hardly knew at the time, summed up Alison so well when he said, 'She has all the good character that I want our two girls to inherit, and so I must learn to give them what Alison would have given them. Amongst these things is her never-ending capacity to forgive and acknowledge others.'

Alison has been one of the finest influences in my life and one for which I am extremely grateful.

Following the *Conquistadores*

When I first began to write this book it had never occurred to me that I might one day actually be teaching in America, let alone become an International Trainer; a grand title for someone who gets to fly around and have fun. I did, however, know when I was first commissioned to do this book that the intention was to publish it simultaneously in the USA and the UK.

I first went to Texas because of an interesting meeting with an American lady. My friends Stan and Rachel brought Virginia to visit us and to have a lesson. She was a very capable rider who had long been disillusioned with the pressures of competition and had thought about giving up riding.

When Virginia told me this I immediately appreciated the feelings she had harboured for so long and noted that they affected both the way she rode and her attitude. Whilst it was obvious that she was very experienced, her seat and indeed her body language generally gave me the impression that she was just going through the motions and not enjoying the opportunity to learn. The first thing I asked her was whether she actually wanted a lesson or merely to play around on a Spanish stallion. When she replied 'Why, a lesson of course' I immediately corrected her seat and told her bluntly to take her hands out of her lap and to sit up. I realized that she was in fact testing me. We did some basic work followed by a little passage and piaffe and finished on a good note. We actually spent more time talking than riding and that continued after the lesson had finished.

The best advice I could give Virginia was to stop considering riding (and indeed life) as a competition, to immerse herself in the art and to learn more from those who truly believed in the classical principles rather than those who either merely pay them lip service or, worse, ignore them completely, wishing only to win. I had obviously helped Virginia a little because, at the end of our discussion, she thanked me, gave me a big hug and went on her way.

I thought I would never see her again but, a short time later, I received a wonderful letter from her that lifted my spirits immensely. She told me that I had changed her life, she was taking her riding seriously again, she was teaching and her search for the true path was well on the way. 'By the way', she added, 'would I go out to Texas to teach?' I jumped at the chance and now Virginia has in turn changed my life.

Wherever the Spanish horse is I find the most passionate, generous, interesting people from the most diverse walks of life, many of whom become my great friends, and America is no exception. There, I have found the most

*An enthusiastic American partnership –
Kathy Graves and Jacto in piaffe.*

warm, welcoming, open-minded people who have a serious desire to learn and work, from the more novice riders right up to those who are competing at the highest levels. They have not only opened their minds but also their hearts and allowed me to do what I love to do: to communicate and inspire.

I can hardly say that I have conquered America but I have grown to love the country and the people who inhabit it, and I look forward to continuing to share my passion for the Spanish horse with them.

PETER MADDISON-GREENWELL

THIS BOOK IS, in a way, a book of two halves, a collaboration of two people who share a love of the Spanish horse but who approach him from slightly differing angles.

My particular interest is the history of the cowboy of the Americas and his working relationship with his horse; it is, however, impossible to understand this fully without acknowledging the indelible impression Spanish horses and horsemanship made upon the American stock industry. My interest in the Spanish horse developed when I was most fortunate to spend two and a half years in Almeria in southern Spain teaching Western riding and escorting rides with horses who carried every possible percentage of Spanish blood!

My contribution to this book has, therefore, been more from the historical angle and, happily, I could bow to Peter's superior knowledge and experience in the training department. We have, nonetheless, worked closely together on all aspects of the book, which, I hope, melds the two halves into a working whole.

JANE LAKE

Introduction

NOWHERE IN THE WORLD has riding dominated and developed in the same way as it has in Spain, where the horse has always been a valued and integral part of a way of life. The Spaniards have never 'used' horses for work, war and pleasure; these occupations simply could not be carried out without horses. As Jan Morris wrote in *Spain*:

> It is a country of horses, from the pampered beauties of the Seville Feria to the tired Rosinantes which…still labour around the Spanish cities with their hackney-carriages. Spain and horses have always gone together…Spaniards love and understand horses…

This inseparability of man and horse is reflected in the fact that the Spanish language makes no distinction between a horseman and a gentleman (or, in medieval times, a knight or nobleman): the word for both is '*caballero*'.

Much has been written about the long history of the Spanish horse, but this book, whilst revealing something of the culture, traditions and ancestral background that have formed this horse's existence, looks particularly at his close relationship with man during many centuries. This relationship is explored from a more up-to-date point of view by looking at what it is like to live and work with the Spanish horse today.

For those of us not born into the world of the Spanish horse, it can take a lifetime to seek out all the information required to understand and appreciate this magnificent creature. For some, a long-standing dream to import a horse from Spain or Portugal can be shattered by a lack of informed preparation and it was for this reason that *Living and Working with the Spanish Horse* was produced.

It is true that if a horse is cared for and trained correctly, then no great problems should arise; but the main stumbling block is that many people do not take into consideration the differences between the training methods and equipment, work, environment and management practices of the Iberian Peninsula and those we in other countries are familiar with. Just the acknowledgement and acceptance of these differences will result in a big step forward in the non-Spanish owner's relationship with the Spanish horse and in a training regime that is enjoyable and successful for both parties.

If we have done our job correctly, then the accumulated knowledge in this book, which is the culmination of many years research, study and experience, will smooth the path of Spanish horse ownership and will help you to develop the kind of relationship that, in so many ways, can only be experienced with the horse of Spain.

Chapter One

The Andalusian Ethos

YOU DO NOT HAVE TO spend much time in Spain before becoming acutely aware of the earthiness, realism, vitality, passion and fire that emerge from the unique culture of the Spanish people. To quote Jan Morris (*Spain*) again, she says of Andalusia: 'There are no half measures in such a place, so close to the earth, so perilously near the frontiers of caricature.'

But, for a great many people, the images of Spain *are* the images of Andalusia:[1] the sun-soaked beaches, the distinctive and varied landscapes, the Moorish architecture, the southern plains and sierras, the black bulls, the horses and elegant horseman and, in particular, the form of song, guitar playing and dance that is usually associated with, and said to originate in, Andalusia – flamenco.[2] Both flamenco and Spanish horses and horsemanship are, in fact, widespread throughout Spain – and indeed in other parts of the world – but they are predominant in Andalusia.

The spirit of true flamenco (as opposed to much of that which is presented to tourists) fills all the senses, bar one: you do not have to touch to feel; it is imbibed through the soul, and it is the soul, the emotions, and a mystical, indefinable 'something' (*duende*) that good flamenco represents.

Although it might be considered to be an overtly romantic view, it could be argued that the inherent musical abilities and truly sensual movement of naturally gifted singers, guitarists and dancers are honed by life experiences influenced by the land and the environment with which the Spanish people are so much in harmony. All the things that evoke flamenco – the moods, contrasts, colour, changing rhythms, and the mix of cultures – appear to echo those of nature.

The brooding mask of a stormy afternoon's night-dark sky counters the delicate complexion of bleached landscapes shimmering in a heat haze under a bleached sky; unimaginably hot winds from Africa or icy, biting blasts from the mountains parry gentle breezes or complete stillness; sombre vultures share the skies with brightly hued bee-eaters, rollers and hoopoes; and the tracks of measured-paced tortoises are crossed by those of darting lizards.

HERE AND OPPOSITE
Views of Andalusia.

The rich colours of terracotta soil; rust-red rain that sweeps in from the Sahara; crimson peppers on white walls vying for space with mauvy-blue wisteria; radiant oranges and yellows of sunsets and the fruit in the citrus groves; the various greens of fertile fields and terraces; and the blues of sea and sky, are all reflected in the costumes of the women dancers and contrast with the monochromatic outfits of the men.

The senses are regaled and beguiled by the soft scent of orange blossom, the calming aroma of shower-soaked herbs, the smell of wood and tobacco smoke, human and equine sweat, and the taste of wine. The drum-like vibration of cicadas and the clicking of equine and caprine hooves on the stones of dry river beds and mountain paths are heard in the percussion of the body, the guitar and the traditional *toque de palmas* and *toqueado* (or *palillos*) – hand-clapping and finger-snapping. (The *castañetas* [castanets] are not considered by some to be representative of true flamenco.)

Rhythm (*compás*) is the lifeblood of flamenco. The extraordinary flamenco rhythms all appear to be at odds with each other, yet they hold a perfect tempo; emotion and passion drive each musical expression in what is seemingly a discordant and unsynchronized way, then it is pulled, held, explored and blended into what is uniquely flamenco.

5

A beautiful collection of Feria dresses, like flowers basking in the bright summer sun.

Every man, woman and child understands, and can participate in, flamenco; they are born with the rhythm in their blood and they all have the ability to hold their own tempo whilst everyone around them breaks into a rhythm of their own. Even thousands of strangers, in a bullring for example, can co-ordinate their clapping rhythms to blend into one harmonious sound. For those who are not Spanish and do not have this inherent ability, but who wish to excel in the Spanish arts, time spent steeped in Spain and its culture is imperative. Some acquire the extra dimension to their work, many do not.

Spanish horses and horsemanship are inextricably woven into this rhythm, this ethos and way of life, and I believe it is this mastery of complicated rhythms that helps Spanish riders, when at their best, to demonstrate complete harmony with a horse and to impart *duende*. Others may struggle for a lifetime to accumulate the immense knowledge required to understand all that a horse can do, only then to realize that somehow they are missing that vital ingredient of harmony, of which rhythm is a major part. How many riders can find the right tempo for their horse's piaffe and stay with that tempo as the horse loses balance and rhythm?

We in many other countries would consider the piaffe, passage and Spanish walk to be advanced movements, but any number of riders in Spain, even the untutored and young children (who are often

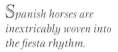

Spanish horses are inextricably woven into the fiesta rhythm.

A *young rider on a stallion – never a second thought! The trusted Spanish stallion will share his power with someone so young, and also care for them all day long.*

dwarfed by the powerful stallions they straddle), can ride a piaffe or passage. By 'untutored' I mean those natural riders who have not been formally trained and who consider themselves neither top trainers nor, often, train in a conventional way. They simply have that innate sense of timing and feel, in the same way that natural dancers know where they should be and what they should do to complement and help their partners and be in time with the music.

Whether or not this is a romanticized view, it is undoubtedly the case that rhythm, harmony, passion and instinct are vital to the understanding of the Spanish horse and Spanish horsemanship.

NOTES

1. The name 'Andalusia' (in Spanish, '*Andalucía*') is derived from 'al-Andalus', the Muslims' empire in Spain, which, from the eighth to the fifteenth centuries AD, consisted of the majority of the Spanish Peninsula. Today, this large southern region of Spain comprises eight provinces: (from west to east) Huelva, Cadiz, Seville, Malaga, Cordoba, Granada, Jaen and Almeria.
2. Flamenco is most widely thought of as the music and dance of the Andalusian Gypsies but it is also said to have been influenced by the music of other peoples on the edges of Spanish society including the Moors and the Jews. In Spanish, one meaning of '*flamenco*' is 'Flemish'. Some Jews migrated to Flanders where they were able to practise their faith and sing their religious songs at will; their less fortunate brethren in Spain called these songs flamenco songs.

Chapter Two

The Legend of Spain

THE SPANISH HORSE, above all others, is a breed that few people, with or without an equestrian background, would not be able to describe, even if it were only artistically or, indeed, a trifle inaccurately. We would all recognize this proud beast (whether from paintings, sculptures, prose, poetry or life) with his upright and alert stance; his almond eyes – the windows to his generous character; his broad chest encasing a big heart; his long, silky mane framing his distinctive head and neck, and draping below long, sloping, flexible shoulders; and his low-set tail that flows straight out of his muscled quarters and trails elegantly behind him like a bride's train when he levades.

The Spanish horse is also identified with legends and myths far more than any other breed. This could be partly because the breed is such an ancient one, partly because of his beauty and bearing, and partly, perhaps, because some horses of the Carthusian type are said to still carry residual bony protuberances on their foreheads. Does the unicorn myth have some basis in fact after all?

Myths, legends and artistic ideals notwithstanding, the Spanish horse has an undoubtedly illustrious history and many books provide excellent, in-depth accounts of the subject. In this book, therefore, only a brief historical breakdown is given. However, because the Spanish horse is considered to be the oldest saddle horse known to man and has a history of domesticity spanning millennia, some examples which illustrate his profound relationship with man are cited.

A Brief History of the Spanish Horse

Prior to the Ice Age, the Iberian Peninsula and Africa were joined by a land bridge over which the primitive, indigenous horses could travel back and forth, making it highly probable that the Andalusian and the Barb have common ancestors. Palaeolithic cave paintings prove the existence of horses in Iberia between 30,000 and 20,000 BC. These paintings depict two distinct types of equine: the northern type had a concave profile; the southern type had a sub-convex profile, and it was the southern horse who would have crossed over to Africa. This primitive horse resembled the Tarpan.

Evidence of domestication first appears in Mesolithic cave paintings depicting horses being led by man in about 5,000–4,000 BC. The descendants of the primitive southern horses were the hardy Sorraia, whose name is derived from the two rivers, the Sor and the Raia, which traverse the Portuguese and Spanish lands these horses inhabited, and join to form one river, the Sorraia.

In the Neolithic Age, horses of oriental (Persian-type) blood were introduced into Iberia by the Phoenicians and North African tribes. Artefacts from this period provide evidence of lances that would have been carried by horsemen (4,000–3,000 BC).

Celtic-Iberian archaeological finds include spurs, bits, horseshoes, lances, shields and saddles (500–200 BC): proof of cavalry activity. Celtic-type horses from the north of the Peninsula interbred with the southern horses, and the Greeks introduced more oriental blood into the mix.

The *Ginetes*

The *Ginetes*[1] were an ancient people who, according to Juan Llamas in his outstanding book *This is the Spanish Horse*, '…had lived in southern Andalusia from time immemorial. We find references to them in Punic works of the sixth century BC.'

The *Ginetes* lived on the plains around the Guadalquivir River in southern Iberia, together with the indigenous horses and bulls they hunted. They became fine horsemen and skilled mounted warriors, whose equestrian abilities and understanding of the wild bulls were passed on to other peoples who conquered and inhabited the Iberian Peninsula. The Tartessions, for example, cultivated the breeding of livestock, and the Iberians developed the use of the bull-wise horses for cattle work, thus bringing about the birth of the ranching industry and the long-standing partnership of the stockman and his horse.

Some interesting questions are posed by the existence of the *Ginetes*. Did they migrate to Africa, taking their equestrian skills with them? If so, then they could be the ancestors of the Berber cavalrymen, the *Zenetes*, who invaded Iberia in the eighth century AD. Did, therefore, the use of the word 'jinete', meaning 'horseman' or 'cavalryman' have its origins in the name of the *Ginetes* rather than the *Zenetes*, as some believe? (The Arabic word '*Zenete*' = '*jinete*'.) It might well have been the *Zenetes* who gave rise to the term '*a la jineta*' (*a la gineta* in Portuguese) for a particular riding style – but which came first, the chicken or the egg?

The *a la jineta* seat was that of the light cavalryman and the stock worker (*vaquero*); both rode with somewhat bent knees and shorter stirrup leathers than were common at the time. The former would have been equipped with a bow and arrow and a light, well-balanced war lance; the latter with a bull-working pole. The warrior relied on his horse to get him in and out of battle quickly by utilizing spurts of speed, quick turns and halts and backing up on command; all moves the *vaqueros* utilized when working cattle.

Influences of Other Peoples

The Romans settled in the Iberian Peninsula in the third century BC, and the Iberian horses they favoured as warhorses were already of a type showing characteristics we would recognize today.

At the beginning of the fifth century AD, the Vandals, and other barbarians, entered Spain from the north and pillaged their way south. The Visigoths, under Roman rule, forced these allied tribes even further south across the straits of Gibraltar (where the land bridge had once been) into North Africa. It can be assumed that the horses the Vandals took with them were of the southern, Sorraia, type because this bloodline has left a recognizable trail. When the Moors arrived in the Iberian Peninsula in AD 711, their Barbs, carrying the blood of the Vandals' horses, were crossed with the native Iberian stock, and produced the jennet,[2] the five-gaited[3] Spanish saddle horses, who were the forebears of the modern Andalusian.

Rodrigo Diaz de Bivar (El Cid[4])

The arrival of the Moors in Iberia presaged a protracted struggle in medieval Spain between Islam and Christianity. A key figure in this struggle was a warrior and folk hero whose relationship with, and love for, his horse are indeed legendary.

Peter Maddison-Greenwell performing a historical display as El Cid riding Cartujano, a Pure-bred Spanish Stallion of old type.

Rodrigo Diaz de Bivar was born in 1043 at Bivar in Castile. When he was a young man, his godfather, a Carthusian monk, allowed him to choose any horse he liked from the monastery's herd. Rodrigo's choice of an unprepossessing, poorly conformed foal disappointed his godfather and he cried, 'Babieca!' ('Idiot!'), but his charge stood by his choice and called the horse 'Babieca'.

Peter Maddison-Greenwell again as El Cid, riding the Spanish Stallion Farolero.

Rodrigo's judgement was, however, upheld when Babieca grew into a fine, strong, courageous warhorse and quickly gained a widespread reputation as his master's formidable partner on the battlefield. Such was their prowess that when Rodrigo offered Babieca to King Alfonso of Leon and Castile, Alfonso refused the horse saying, 'God forbid that I should take him…for you and this horse have brought us great honour.'

In earlier years, however, Rodrigo had fought against Alfonso in the army of Alfonso's brother, Sancho. On Sancho's death, Alfonso exiled Rodrigo, accusing him of plotting against the Crown. As a result, he became a mercenary and sold his services to the Muslim leaders until Alfonso, fearful of the Muslim invasion, persuaded Rodrigo to fight for him again. But, in the years that followed, Rodrigo fought as an independent military leader.

His final triumph was capturing Valencia from the Moors after a long siege. Having been mortally wounded during one of his many skirmishes outside the city, and knowing nothing could be done for him, his last command was that his body be secured upon Babieca and that they should be sent out against the Moors. For the last time Babieca led the charge, and the Moors, believing that 'El Cid' had been raised from the dead, fled in panic.

Rodrigo was buried at the Monastery of San Pedro de Cardeña, and when Babieca died two years later at the age of forty, he was rewarded for his many years of loyal service by being buried next to his comrade-in-arms as Rodrigo had requested. After the Peninsular War, their remains, plus those of Rodrigo's wife, Doña Ximena, were moved to the Catedral de Santa Maria in Burgos, where they lie today. A statue of El Cid mounted on Babieca dominates the city of Burgos.

There are no definite details of Babieca's breeding as there were neither Spanish stud books nor registers at the time, but his great courage, strength, stamina and conformational characteristics are those which are held in high esteem in modern Andalusians.

The Iberian Horse in Medieval Conflict

During the 500 years of the Middle Ages, the Iberian horse was making his presence felt throughout the world as the fast, agile, hot-blooded and elegant Spanish charger ridden *a la jineta* by Spanish and Portuguese light cavalrymen, and coveted by royalty and noblemen. The other warhorse of this era was the slower, phlegmatic, cold-blooded heavier horse ridden *a la brida* by the armour-plated knights. *A la brida* was the second seat of which all good Iberian horseman of the time were expected to be masters: the legs were dropped long and braced forward and the backside was braced against the cantle of the *brida* (war) saddle.

King Duarte of Portugal (1401–38), wrote a treatise entitled, in English, *The book to teach to ride well in all saddles.* Duarte was a proponent of the *jineta* seat; he recognized that the way to defeat the Moors on the battlefield was to use the Iberian light cavalry riding *a la jineta*, like the Moors, and these cavalrymen would have greater success than the *brida* horsemen.

In the fifteenth century, the Carthusian monks from Cartuja in Jerez, elected themselves protectors of what they felt was the true Spanish riding style: *a la jineta*; and threatened those who chose to ride *a la brida* with excommunication. These monks (whose interest in the Spanish horse reached, as we have seen, back to the time of El Cid), were also the first to organize a breeding programme. Starting with a very few horses, they kept a cloak of secrecy around their selective breeding work. For centuries they maintained the original bloodlines of their Carthusian (*Cartujano*) horses, retaining the smaller size, and eliminated, as far as possible, out-crosses with other breeds.

The New World

Just as the Moors were being ousted from the Iberian Peninsula in 1492, the Spaniards were making their first forays into the New World. The *Conquistadores* of the sixteenth century rode a *la jineta* into the new lands on their Spanish jennets, horses who founded a fine Hispanic dynasty in South, Central and North America, the best known of which are the Criollos, Crioulos, Peruvian Pasos, Paso Finos, Chickasaws and Mustangs. Some of these horses are famous for their extra gaits, demonstrating their five-gaited ancestry; and many still carry the characteristic primitive colours and markings of the Sorraia, i.e. yellow and blue duns with black eel stripes down the back and black 'zebra' marks on the legs.

The majority of the *Conquistadores* came from the cattle-raising area of Estremadura, a parched and unmerciful land that produced men who were hardy and iron-willed in the extreme; traits that were found in equal measure in their horses. These horses survived months crossing the Atlantic exposed to the unforgiving elements; their only way to sustain any form of fitness, it was said, was to perform piaffe in the tight spaces on the open decks of the small Spanish sailing ships. On arrival in the New World, the horses were disembarked by being plunged into the sea to swim to shore. These tough, brave little horses had been used for war and stock work in their homeland and they reprised these roles in the New World. The conquest would have been untenable without them and they were the *Conquistadores'* strongest link to survival.

The human/horse relationship is going to be extremely deep when you depend on another being as much as the New World Spaniards depended on their horses. A well-known and frequently quoted phrase from the annals of the Conquest is: 'For, after God, we owed the victory to the horses.' In *The Horses of the Conquest*, R. B. Cunninghame Graham expands upon this:

> If the Conquistadores (after God) owed their conquest to the horses, there was an intimate companionship between them that is well-nigh impossible to understand to-day.

A companionship and pride at the same time, such as a man may feel for a younger brother who has accompanied him in some adventure.

This love of horses pervaded every class and all conditions of the Spaniards at the time.

There was another way in which the horses helped the victory. The Conquistadores were seen as god-like apparitions, half-man/half-horse, and instilled fear into otherwise immensely brave native warriors. The Spaniards displayed their horsemanship, moving as one with their horses, galloping towards their opponents, then turning or stopping suddenly and impressively; the impact might not have had the same effect had they been lesser horsemen who bounced about in the saddle desperately trying to find their balance!

The inheritors of the Spanish horses, cattle, riding style and ranching acumen in the Americas never lost this affinity with the horse. Indeed, the *vaqueros, llaneros, gauchos, huasos* and cowboys also inherited the Spanish horseman's idea that heaven would not be complete if horses were not there too. The *gauchos*, it seems, did not even require a very quiet time in their heaven, Trapalanda – a paradise of lush green grass and abundant, crystal-clear water – because, if this word stems from the Spanish verb '*trapalear*' which means '(of a horse) to clatter, beat its hooves, clip-clop' (*Collins Spanish Dictionary* 1985), then peace was not an option; the presence of the horse was far more important.

The horse was a companion, a lifeline, an essential part of life; far less indispensable than women. Edward Larocque Tinker gives two extracts – the second being delightfully politically incorrect, by today's standards – from South American songs that demonstrate a man's depth of feeling for his horse (only the English translations have been given here). The first is from a Pampas ballad:

> My horse was my life,
> My goods, my only treasure.

The second is from a Venezuelan *llanero*'s ballad:

> My horse and my mate
> died at the same time.
> To the Devil with the woman!
> It's my horse I miss.

Even the cowboys of nineteenth-century North America were not immune to the emotions aroused by the death of a, probably, 'plug-ugly' and dubious-tempered, Mustang workmate and a loved companion, as this often-quoted epitaph proves.

Here lies 'What Next'
Born _____ , 1886, at _____ .
Died July 16, 1892, near Ft. Washakie, Wyo.
He had the Body of a Horse,
The Spirit of a Knight, and
The Devotion of the Man
Who Erected this Stone.

The Renaissance Onward

To revert to European history, the Renaissance period saw changes of attitude to a great many things; it was an era of enlightenment, a period of flamboyance, art and great pageantry; and the art of training horses also experienced its own Renaissance.

A key figure at the start of this era was Charles I of Spain (1516–1556), who was also Emperor Charles V of a region that included what is now Austria. He was a highly respected equestrian whose love for the Spanish horse and the *jineta* style of riding had a very strong influence throughout his domain. Spanish horses were first imported into the Austrian region by Charles' brother, Ferdinand, and provided the base stock for the development of the Lipizzaner breed. It is, therefore, easy to see why the Spanish Riding School of Vienna is so named.

Born in the year before Charles I died, the Frenchman Antoine de Pluvinel (1555–1620) was one of the founding fathers of the Renaissance style of equitation. He used reward and praise to achieve results when training, in preference to the often cruel methods of some former trainers. His methods were published posthumously in 1629 in his book *L'Instructions de Roi*, which was based upon the lessons he gave to Louis XIII. Both this king and Louis XIV were admirers of the Spanish horse.

The English nobleman, William Cavendish, Duke of Newcastle (1592–1676), was riding master to the then Prince of Wales, later to become Charles II. With Cromwell's victory in the Civil War, Newcastle, a Royalist, was forced into exile, as was the future king. In Antwerp, Newcastle learnt the methods for training horses in the art of the high school and opened his famed riding academy. Like

Pluvinel, he developed his own methods, which were pub-lished in his book *Methode et Invention Nouvelle de Dresser les Chevaux*; which was rendered into English as *A General System of Horsemanship*. Newcastle also esteemed the Spanish horse above all others, stating in his book that the breed is:

> …the noblest horse in the world…the most beautiful that can be…he is of great spirit and courage, and docile, hath the proudest walk, the proudest trot and the best action in his trot; the loftiest gallop, the swiftest careers and is the lovingest and gentlest horse and fittest of all for a king in the day of his triumph…much more intelligent than even the best Italian horses, and for that reason the easiest dressed, because they observe so much with their eyes and their memories are so good.

Born twelve years after Newcastle's death, the Frenchman François Robichon de la Guérinière (1688–1751) opened a riding academy in Paris in 1715; he was later entrusted with the Académie des Tuileries, where he remained as director until his death. It was Guérinière who developed the shoulder-in, the move-ment that is the foundation for all exercises of collection. Guérinière's book, *Ecole de Cavalerie (School of Horsemanship)*, published in 1729, is believed to have influenced the training methods of the famous Riding Schools of Vienna, Saumur and Hanover since that time. The engravings in this book depict horses of a distinctly Spanish type performing the school movements.

These vastly influential figures clearly held the Spanish horse in high regard and, with the establishment of formal riding schools throughout Europe during the fifteenth to nineteenth centuries, he had all the qualities required to take him to the top of the class. His courage, strength, gentleness and small stature (on average 15 hh) combined with a well-muscled, close-coupled, clean-limbed conformation meant that he was perfectly suited to the collection required for the high-school movements. Many of the fast turns, sudden stops, leaps and movements on the spot initially so important to sur-vival on the battlefield, and when working cattle, developed into an artistic form of equitation that culminated in the classical dressage of the finest riding academies in Europe.

Influence on Other Breeds

Notwithstanding the jealousy with which the Carthusian monks had histor-ically guarded the *Cartujano* bloodlines, Spanish blood has a long record of being much in demand to improve other stock, its influence being by no

Scenes from the old riding school at Bolsover Castle, home of the Duke of Newcastle.

Danielle Lawniczak in seventeenth-century costume on the Tres Sangres stallion, Saeta.

FAR LEFT *Danielle and Saeta with a friend, Diane Hesketh.*

LEFT *Peter Maddison-Greenwell and daughter, Katie, in seventeenth-century costume. Peter is riding the Hispano Arabe, Chico.*

means confined to famous studs such as those at Kladrub and Lipizza. For example, back in the twelfth century, whilst travelling through Wales, Archbishop Baldwin observed:

> In…Powys, there are some excellent studs put apart for breeding, and deriving their origin from some fine Spanish horses, which Robert de Belesme, Earl of Shrewsbury, brought into this country…the horses sent from hence are remarkable for their majestic proportion and astonishing fleetness.

The virtues of these horses obviously had a protracted influence on the Shrewsbury dynasty since, some two centuries later, the then Earl is known to have followed in the footsteps of his ancestor by importing Spanish stallions; he infused their blood with that of the native ponies and the resultant cross became known as the Powys Cob, from which the Welsh Cob developed.

There is a view that Spanish blood may have had a more accidental influence on another breed native to the British Isles. In 1588, some ships of the Spanish Armada were wrecked off the Irish coast and there are those who believe that the Spanish horses who managed to swim ashore were predominant in the development of the Connemara pony. This is not proven but, certainly, Irish merchants traded with Spain and they may have imported horses who were then crossed with indigenous stock. It is also possible that in even earlier times the Celtic peoples of Ireland brought Spanish stock in.

A much more fully documented injection of Spanish blood into British stock took place in the seventeenth century, after George Villiers, Duke of Buckingham and connoisseur of outstanding horses, became Master of the Horse to James I in 1616. Whilst negotiating the marriage between Prince Charles and the Infanta of Spain, Buckingham managed to acquire some of the finest Spanish horses bred in the Royal Cordoban stud for both himself and the English crown, despite the fact that the marriage arrangements subsequently collapsed.

From his own marriage to the daughter of the Earl of Rutland, Buckingham gained an estate at Helmsley in North Yorkshire in close proximity to the area of Cleveland where the famed pack horses, the Chapman horses, were bred. Local breeders made good use of the services of Buckingham's Spanish stallions, and thus he had a great influence on the Cleveland Bay, the breed that developed from the Spanish/Chapman cross. Buckingham's stallions were not the sole influence, however; other Spanish and Barb stallions arriving at the port of Whitby would also have left their mark on the Cleveland Bay.

The Spanish horse enjoyed his place as 'the first horse of Europe' for many centuries and only started to take a lesser role with the growing popularity of the faster, leggier horses who would develop into the modern Thoroughbred. However, the strength of his genes meant that he still had a great influence on the 'blood' horses of the world. In the eighteenth century, one of the foundation stallions of the Thoroughbred was a Barb, the Godolphin Barb, and, as has been discussed, Barbs, in all probability, carry Spanish blood. In addition, a great many of the best-quality mares put to the foundation stallions and their offspring would have carried Spanish blood.

Back across the Atlantic, in the middle of the eighteenth century, English blood stallions were imported by the American colonists and crossed with the

An interesting example of Spanish blood in America – Valiente Corazon, a registered Azteca. The Azteca breed registry is made up of horses who are at least 50 % Andalusian, the rest of the blood being American Quarter Horse. Valiente Corazon is ¾ Andalusian, being by the Andalusian stallion Davidoso de le Parra out of an Aztecan mare who was 50 % Andalusian and 50 % Quarter Horse. Valiente Corazon is owned by Kathy Graves and is ridden here by Peter Maddison-Greenwell's American friend, Brooke Crampton.

Chickasaw Indian ponies of Spanish jennet descent to produce the quarter-mile sprinters known as 'Quarter Pathers' or 'Quarter Running Horses'. When the pioneers moved out to the Western lands, their Quarter Horses were infused with further Spanish blood and 'cow savvy' by the Mustangs of the plains, thus taking the breed a little closer to its roots. And in more recent years the Mexicans have crossed the Quarter Horse with the Andalusian to produce the Azteca, the only New World horse to descend directly from the modern Andalusian as opposed to the modern Andalusian's ancestors.

Thankfully, horses are no longer required to take a part in men's petty arguments or greater battles but, over the centuries, the Spanish horse has more than proved his worth in this field; his genes are to be found in innumerable breeds and types, and he is the embodiment of the stock horse as well as the finest exponent of true classical equitation. It must surely be safe to say that this is a history and reputation to be proud of; he is indeed the Legend of Spain.

Notes

1. Also 'Cinetes' or 'Cynetes'.
2. 'Jennet' is also derived from the word 'jinete'.
3. The gaits included the four-beat gait known as ambling.
4. 'El Cid' was the Spanish version of the Arabic name given to Rodrigo Diaz de Bivar by the Moors: 'al-sid', meaning 'the lord'. The Spanish also called him 'El Campeador', 'the champion'.

Chapter Three

Doma Vaquera – the Art of the Stockman

THE GENESIS OF THE stockman's art is summed up to perfection by Juan Llamas in his book, *This is the Spanish Horse*: 'Out in the country, many centuries ago, among the *Ginetes, la doma vaquera* was born, and subjected to the exigencies proper to an art in which life and death are but two sides of the same coin'.

The essential art of the mounted stockman, or cowboy, is the ability to work cattle quietly, safely and efficiently, and to do that well he needs a highly trained equine partner. In Spain, *la doma vaquera* encompasses the finely honed and precise skills of the stockman and his horse – whether they are performed on the ranches or in the competitive arena. The work of the *vaquera* rider is fascinating. True *vaquera* riders are like the country, gritty and tough, and they must be strong, resourceful and resilient. They are by nature hard-working, hard-playing men, full of passion and love for their horses and their bulls; and a more sporting, honourable and generous breed of mankind you will never meet.

The definition of '*doma*' is 'dressage' (from the French verb '*dresser*': to dress or train a horse), thus *la doma vaquera* could be said to be the dressage of the stockman.

'*Vaquero*'[1] means 'cowboy' but I prefer to think of these industrious and honourable men of Spain – and the Americas – as stockmen because, unfortunately, in England in particular, the word 'cowboy' has become a derogatory term for a shoddy workman.

On unfenced land, man and horse have to display the epitome of control in the movements which are part of their everyday work; this control is essential when working the bulls. The *vaquera* rider is neither always attractive nor necessarily elegant, and not every rider or horse will have what it takes to make a Spanish champion. But that which many competition-dressage riders struggle to do with both hands on the reins in the quiet serenity of a level, well-marked-out arena, the stockmen will perform as a matter of course on hard, rough ground and in relentless heat. The execution and timing of their passes, turns on the haunches and the forehand, changes of leg, half-pirouettes, reining back and exact and immediate halts, would be the envy of many a dressage competitor.

Time appears to stand still in the ranch country of Spain; tractors, four-wheel-drive vehicles and quad bikes have not replaced the horse there. The stockman still saddles his horse, mounts up and rides out to tend the cattle with the same type of tack (see Chapter 7) and work methods as his predecessors have used for centuries. And his senses, so finely tuned to pick up every minute change in nature's sounds, sights and smells, will not be offended by the strident ring-tone of a mobile phone, glaring graffiti, or exhaust fumes.

Many *vaquera* riders still train their horses in the same way their fathers and grandfathers did (see Chapter 9) and, although some of their methods may appear somewhat crude to many, it must be remembered that there are good and bad trainers and riders in every equestrian field. Life in the country can still be harsh, and the working horses are not ridden purely for pleasure; they have a job, a potentially dangerous job, to do and the safety and well-being of both horse and rider are at stake. If a horse is brought to a halt a little more abruptly or turned a little more forcefully than would normally be acceptable, because he is in danger of being caught by the horns of a bad-tempered bull, then it is far more forgivable than doing the same when a horse simply has to carry out the less life-threatening activities of halting at X or turning down the school at A.

When the *vaquera* horse and rider work in rhythm and relaxed harmony, however, the partnership is inspirational; the obedience and submissiveness of the horse – responding to every request willingly and alertly, and with every ounce of energy – are matched by the rider's understanding and appreciation.

Doma vaquera work has also found its way into the competition arena where it is seen not only all over Spain but also in many other places around the world.

For spectators, the element of excitement is added to those of the art of ultimate control and speed. In just six minutes the competitor must demonstrate a series of movements at both walk and *galope* (canter and full gallop)[2]

– the trot is not used – using only one hand on the reins, this bridle hand being traditionally the left hand. A switch, or whip, which is held upright, is used only in demonstrations and not in competition.

At the walk, the rider's right hand is placed on the right thigh, with the palm of the hand over the hip joint; the fingers are held together with the first finger running down the trouser seam and the thumb placed just below the groin crease. At the canter, the hand, with the fingers closed but relaxed, is placed in front of the chest as though holding a switch or, perhaps, when a couple are parading at a fiesta, the hand of a lover who sits behind her man with both her legs on the nearside (*a la grupa*) and her dress tucked under her backside and covering the side of the horse's quarters.

A la grupa *at a fiesta.*

The movements executed start with simple circles at collected and extended walk, turns on the haunches and forehand, halt and rein-back and the *apoyos* (half-passes).

The *vaquera* walk is of particular importance; it must show good forward movement demonstrating a strong desire to get somewhere, and have a rhythm that sets the *mosquera* (fly fringe) swinging to left and right across the horse's face like a silent metronome. This indicates that the horse is walking 'through' from behind with a fluent and regular swing.

Rider and horse must then move into the canter at the prescribed moment, without hesitation, and proceed to perform the more difficult movements: passes, turns, demi-pirouettes, pirouettes, canter to halt, rein-back to canter. The work becomes increasingly demanding; the pirouettes can be fast and are often doubled, that is, a pirouette is ridden in one direction, the leg is changed, and the horse pirouettes back in the other direction, without leaving the spot. The test always finishes with a dramatic full gallop to halt, often with repeated combinations of rein-back to gallop to halt.

This sport that celebrates the work of the stockman is hard work for the rider and especially demanding for the horse, which is probably why a team of judges that includes a vet must inspect the horses before and after the test. The horse must not exhibit any signs of abuse; a critical look at the horse's flanks will expose any excessive use of spur; blood must not be drawn. At least in Spain abuse with rowelled spurs is exposed by bleeding, and a rider can be

Adoma vaquera
competitor ready
for action.

penalized. Abuse elsewhere with the blunt, rounded spurs used in other disciplines – the bruising, worn-away hair and the horse's reaction when the spurs are applied – might not be so immediately obvious, or penalized.

The judges also have to check that the traditional clothing and tack are correct. The rider's hair must look neat under the hat and, for some reason, no *vaquera* rider I have seen wears facial hair when competing.

(Some years ago I had been invited to present a trophy at a national qualifier competition in Alcala de los Galzules. It was the night before the competition and I was enjoying a drink with several of the country's champion *vaquera* riders, when one of them decided I needed a shave. At the time I was sporting what I thought was a rather fetching military moustache, as you can see from the picture of the presentation the next day. It took several of them to hold me down across a bar table whilst the instigator pulled out an alarmingly large sporting knife. Fortunately they were just fooling around and left my moustache intact. On returning home I removed the moustache and it has stayed off ever since.)

Although *la doma vaquera* has made a successful transition to the competition arena, it is in the country, in the domain of the fighting bull, where the circle of the relationship between the stockman and his horse is unbroken: 'Horse and rider, always together, two lives with a single destiny…' (Juan Llamas, *This is the Spanish Horse*).

Peter Maddison-Greenwell (still attached to his moustache) presents an award at a major *vaquera competition.*

La Garrocha

> I want you to be a *garrochista*,
> I want you to be a gentleman,
> born of the earth itself,
> as good countrymen are.

These four lines (translated from the Spanish) are from an impressive and moving poem by Miguel Higueros that describes a father's wish for his son to follow in his footsteps. To carry the *garrocha* (the bull-working pole/spear/ lance) into the country, to work the stock, to test the bulls, is a large and important part of the Spanish stockman's life. This tradition is so strong in the Spanish stockman's world, that a man would be very proud to be given the title of *garrochista*.

The wooden *garrocha* has a metal point at one end, is generally 14 ft (4.27 m) long and its diameter widens to the size of a hand grasp at the top end. Its use can be demonstrated in two ways: it is a tool which helps to get the tough job of working the bulls done, but the *garrocha* can also be used as part of an artistic display.

This photograph, taken at the biggest show in Spain, emphasizes the fact that young boys are still encouraged to follow the path of the garrochista.

The *garrochista's* work is part of the *vaquera* training. The rider must be able to ask the horse to perform all the movements required using only one hand on the reins: the left, or bridle, hand, thus freeing the right hand to handle the *garrocha*. The rein aids must, of course, be given in conjunction with the seat and leg aids, and the voice is also used, but not in competition. To carry out this work, the natural body aids must become extremely refined. Communication with the horse has to become second nature; a *garrochista* must focus on the use of the *garrocha* in much the same way as driving a car should be practically automatic so that the greater part of your concentration is on the road and other road users. Good exponents of the *garrochista's* art will use the *garrocha* as an extension of their own body.

LEFT *Jesus Morales – this fantastic, inspirational rider was the first Peter Maddison-Greenwell saw perform with the* garrocha *whilst riding without his hands on the reins.*

Another expert example of the garrochista's *art.*

Acoso y Derribo

The term *acoso y derribo* means 'pursue and bring down', and it is all about the testing of the young bulls' courage, tenacity and ferocity to see if they are of the right calibre for the bullring. The Spanish black bulls are renowned for their mettle and the breeder selects carefully the stock to be presented for the challenge; a challenge that is also a test of the courage and stamina of the *vaquera* horses and their riders.

Two riders, one on each side of the young bull, steer him down a long, straight line at the gallop and, at the right moment, the *garrochista* uses the end of the *garrocha* to unbalance the bull or bring him down. The character of the bull is judged by his expression, courage and fighting spirit in returning to his feet and refusing to be beaten. It is a point of pride for the breeder to put forward only the very best of his stock for the bullring.

The Use of the *Garrocha* as an Art Form

Performers of this art form work freestyle; they can present any movements they like that show off their skill with the *garrocha*. A performance will probably include all the lateral work, turns, changes of leg and pirouettes seen in a *doma vaquera* competition, and often at speed that defies belief.

Some years ago I saw a display by Sebastian Fernandes. It started at a slow, rhythmical walk, with just a few simple and artistic turns around, then under, the *garrocha*, and then progressed to a series of breathtaking spins under the pole. The movements and shapes created were artistic, almost balletic and, as with ballet, the beauty of a performance hides the amount of agility, strength and stamina required by the performers.

More recently I witnessed another outstanding display. The rider entered the arena with the *garrocha* carried on his right shoulder, took off his hat with his left hand and began a remarkable performance. His horse moved forward in a piaffe-like way, making several turns on the haunches both under and away from the *garrocha*. Each turn was a single movement, a graceful lift of the forehand, a 180 degree turn and a soft return to the ground: a *media vuelta* (see Chapter 9). Each turn coiled the horse like a spring until he could contain his energy no longer and he burst into a courbette, rising onto his hind legs, his front legs tucked in tight, and springing straight into the air, as if to smell the sky. As the music picked up tempo, the pair leapt into gallop. The performance was astounding and all the more so because the rider had no hands on the reins: the reins were tied to his belt in the same way that a *rejoneador's* reins would be when he requires two hands for the *banderillas*.

LIVING AND WORKING WITH THE HORSE OF SPAIN

These performances inspired me to acquire the *garrochista's* skills, including working with no hands on the reins. In time, with my horse Chico's invaluable help and a few directional mishaps, I achieved my goals and use my *Fantasia a la Garrocha* routine to show this extraordinary equestrian art to a wider audience.

Peter Maddison-Greenwell and Farolero practising garrocha technique in the English countryside – something the locals are not yet used to.

Peter Maddison-Greenwell on Farolero, performing with the garrocha. In the picture above they are accompanied by the famous flamenco dancer, El Moreno ('The Dark One').

BELOW Close display work by a group of garrochistas at a major show in Spain.

I am a traditionalist and feel very strongly that certain facets of cultures should be upheld. The *garrocha* is a tool that is an important part of a culture with a very long history, and, if only for this reason, it should be treated with respect. It is not a white bendy pole called a *garrocho* to be used as a so-called training aid, as I was horrified to see it portrayed in an English riding magazine.

The *Rejoneador* – Warrior or Artist?

The role of the *rejoneador* is defined by Edward Laroque Tinker in his book *Centaurs of Many Lands*: 'The *rejoneador*, it must be explained, is a mounted man who fights bulls and does, on horseback, everything the matador does, including the killing.'

In the time of the Moorish occupation, young Spanish noblemen adopted the Moors' sport of hunting the wild bulls in open country with a lance (*rejón*). This was the sport of wealthy amateurs; only young men of means owned horses good enough to enable them to participate in the sport, which soon found its way into enclosed arenas so that audiences would be safe.

Laroque Tinker records:

> Tauromachy continued to be the sport of gentleman amateurs until the advent of the Bourbon kings, who seriously disapproved of the art and discouraged it. In the face of their censure, the young courtiers and noblemen could not continue to indulge in their favorite sport. As a consequence, their place in the bullring was taken by paid plebeians, who made it a profession, and fought on foot because they could not afford horses and did not know how to ride them. So, for generations, *rejoneo* became a neglected art, until it was again revived by Antonio Cañero about 1920.

A *rejoneador* takes the *doma vaquera* skills to the ultimate conclusion; he chooses to ride his horse into a contest with one of the fiercest beasts on earth using the *rejón* and the *banderillas* to do battle against the bull's lethal horns. Even if you have strong feelings about the tradition of bullfighting, the horse's unparalleled courage and the rider's immense skill cannot be denied. Without these qualities, neither would survive long without serious injury or death. Whilst we all take a calculated, usually insured, risk each time we enter the arena, we are seldom presented with the same immediate fear of facing the powerful and awesome opponent that is the Spanish black bull.

The bullring has, in a comparatively short time, become one of the most important facets of Spanish culture (its heyday probably being in the eighteenth century) and it is probably the most controversial. It is difficult for those of us who are not brought up in this culture to understand why a man would willingly stand before probable death in such away. It is, therefore, no surprise that the *rejoneador*, like the matador and picador, are deeply religious. They, like the breeders, also have a respect, even a love, for the bull, and have written poetry and songs bestowing many virtues upon the bull, not least of which is courage.

Let me give you an outline of the *corrida* (bullfight). The matador, who fights the bull on foot, welcomes the bull into the arena by making a few passes with a large cape; usually these are the basic cape passes called *verónicas*, which were named after the woman who offered Christ a cloth on the way to his crucifixion. Next, the picadors ride in to the bullring on horses protected by heavy padding, in order to take on the dangerous task of preparing the bull for the matador by goading him with their lances. The matador then weakens the bull's neck with the *banderillas*, thus lowering his head.

That which follows is a *pas de deux* for matador and bull. The matador barely moves from his chosen spot in the bullring, encouraging his dangerous dance partner to charge, which the bull does, following the cape as it is taken artistically in front of the horns and around the matador. The man stands tall and arrogant, his back arched, his chest up, head high; his *traje de luces* ('suit of lights') sparkling in the late sun in stark contrast with the solid, matt-black mass of fighting bull. The 'moment of truth', the kill, must be executed correctly, swiftly and with respect for a worthy opponent.

This differs from the way in which the *rejoneador* must fight the bull. First he must challenge the bull to charge, and in order to keep ahead of the bull when he is at his freshest, the *rejoneador* rides a fast, rangy horse; probably a Spanish/Arab cross or Spanish/Thoroughbred cross (see Chapter 5). At every opportunity the *rejoneador* places a *banderilla* between the bull's shoulder blades, each one of which weakens the bull. The incredible power of this formidable beast is never more obvious than when pitted against a horse and rider.

As the fight progresses the *rejoneador* changes to a more compact, agile, and braver, horse – probably a Pure-bred Spanish or Lusitano – for this is the horse who must get close to the bull when he is at his most angry and fierce. This is surely the last bastion of war on horseback; the *rejoneador* must be able to trust his mount as much as the cavalrymen of former years had to trust their horses. His knowledge of the enemy, his horsemanship and his years of training are finely honed into the epitome of control and skill you will seldom see outside the bullring.

A half-pass at the canter in a dressage competition has a grace and rhythm of its own, but in this situation, when 500 kilos of blood, muscle and bone are bearing down on you, a gallop virtually on the spot, a half-pass change to half-pass, as the horse feigns direction and the bull passes within a hair's breadth, is a matter of life and death. With the reins tied to his belt, the *rejoneador* must place two final *banderillas* simultaneously between the bull's shoulder blades. He then surges away before the bull, pirouetting time and time again in front of the horns as if in celebration. The *rejón de muerte* delivers the 'moment of truth'.

Views from the bullring.

There is skill and artistry in the way the battle is fought. There is courage on all sides: man, mount and beast. Occasionally the bull wins and is honoured and turned out to pasture. Even when he loses, his life has been better than that of many animals. He is allowed to grow in a natural way in a herd in the vast expanses of the most beautiful parts of southern Spain. He will live until five years of age and die a death that has more respect and honour than a great many of his counterparts bred purely for meat in other places. So think carefully before you condemn the *corrida*.

It is considered by some today that the Lusitano (see Chapter 8) has a greater aptitude for the *rejoneo* than the Andalusian – because the Portuguese have bred selectively for the bullring, whilst many Spanish breeders have concentrated on the Andalusian's beauty – and both Spanish and Portuguese *rejoneadors* ride Lusitanos. The famous Opus was a Lusitano, although he is said by some to have been born in Arcos de la Frontera in Spain. He is of Veiga bloodlines; fiery and fantastic. Astride Opus, Alvaro Domecq shone as a master of the art of the *rejoneo* and showed his genius in the saddle. Opus could gallop on the spot and backwards, and was totally focused on the bull. Anyone watching this partnership could only envy the skill, courage and sheer mastery of movement.

There are relatively few *rejoneadors* in Spain and they often come from well-known horse- and bull-breeding families. They are born to the bullring and, like their stock, carefully nurtured and trained; for this is an occupation that has serious risks, a mistake is not judged in points but in broken bones or loss of life itself. If you get it wrong in the dressage arena you may lose two points; in the bullring you could gain two points!

Today it is not just the famous breeding dynasties, such as the Domecqs or Bohorquez, who hand down the mantle of *rejoneador* from father to son. There are others who pit their unquestionable courage and skill in this dance with death.

1. The Spanish masculine noun 'vaquero' means cowboy or stockman, and as an adjective it means 'in the style of' or 'belonging to' a cowboy or stockman. In Spanish, however, the gender of the ending of an adjective agrees with the gender of the ending of the noun; thus as 'doma' is a feminine noun, in *la doma vaquera*, the adjective is 'vaquera' and not 'vaquero'.
2. The word canter is relatively modern and is used primarily by English-speaking riders. Even so, this gait was once always known as the gallop and in many languages this relationship remains obvious. For example, the French use the term 'un petit galop', ('small gallop') to describe the canter; the Spanish still use the term 'galope' for canter and for a full gallop.

Chapter Four

Doma Clasica – from Purpose to Pure Beauty

T HE DEBATE ABOUT WHAT classical riding is, or should be, would constitute a book in its own right, but in this book we talk about *doma clasica* from its roots in war to what it means generally in Spain today. Dressage today is often considered to be simply another type of equestrian competition, but it should be much more than that. Classical dressage should be the enlightened and understanding training of a horse, which helps him to achieve the level of education that is right for him and for the sphere in which he will be used. Not all horses are destined to be high-flyers and outstanding performers, but there is no reason why the classical principles championed by historical and modern masters cannot be applied to the training of every horse and pony.

As stated in Chapter 3, '*doma*' is the Spanish word for dressage (that is, training) and in Spain, *doma clasica* is manège, or school, riding as opposed to *doma vaquera*, or country, riding.

We can see the epitome of classical dressage demonstrated by the Royal Andalusian School of Equestrian Art, the Portuguese School of Equestrian Art, the Spanish Riding School of Vienna and the Cadre Noir in Saumur. These are the last strongholds of classical riding as we know it today. There are, however, some truly passionate ambassadors of classical riding who work outside the auspices of these academies but who make every attempt to adhere to the academies' principles; some are able to execute not only good classical movements but can also perform the 'airs above the ground', or at least some of them.

Danielle Lawniczak on the Pure-bred Spanish stallion, Pasodoble, performing doma clasica.

A doma clasica *pair performing at Olympia. Nearer camera: Lorri Ould on Zurito. Behind: Michelle Enoch on Navindeño.*

There are also those who give poor renditions of the classical movements and then have the audacity to pronounce the movements to be correct. For example, I have seen many levades that are no more than haphazard rears; piaffes performed with shuffling hind legs; and passage-like movements that vaguely resemble a bunny hopping on three legs.

If you examine the various movements from the basic lateral work to the more advanced airs, you can see how so many of them had a real purpose in work and war. And with these activities in mind, the first principle you must understand is that, for both, the horse had to be ridden with one hand, the left, as the right hand was needed to throw a spear, wield a sword, fire a gun, open a gate, rope a steer, or carry a *garrocha*.

The performance by the solo rider in the displays by the Spanish Riding School is one of the finest demonstrations of this. The rider enters the arena, salutes, holds his switch in the right hand as if it was an upturned sword, and proceeds to execute every air, or movement, on the ground. His hand remains in the same position while he rides piaffe, passage, half-passes in passage, tempi changes, and pirouettes – including full pirouettes in piaffe.

Further to these movements on the ground, there are a number of airs above the ground which are seldom seen in any comprehensive form outside the aforementioned academies. These airs are truly wonderful demonstrations of control, agility, balance and pure power. For ease of description, I will categorize the movements as follows.

Movements when the Horse is Balancing on his Hind Legs

The levade is developed from a slow, precipitated piaffe, a gradual lift of the forehand until the front legs are held up together; the hind legs should be well under the body with the lower legs flexed at the hock joints to the point where the hocks are very nearly on the ground. The angle of the horse's back should be approximately 30 degrees to the ground.

With the pesade, the bend in the hind legs is not as deep as with the levade and the horse's back should be at an angle of 45 degrees. This air follows the same criteria as the levade and should show the same elements of ease of control and grace to be considered classical. A rear with both front legs apart is perfectly acceptable in the stunt world when the horse is trained to perform this on cue and, when done properly, it is to be appreciated, but it is a rear, not a pesade.

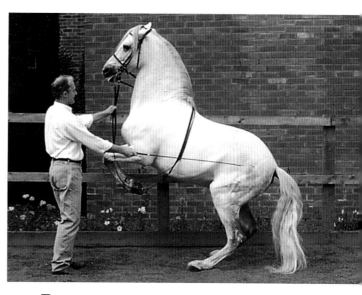

ABOVE *Peter Maddison-Greenwell training Cartujano to perform the pesade in-hand. If there was a little more flexion in the joints of the hind legs, and Cartujano's back was at a slightly more acute angle to the ground, this would become a levade.*

Peter Maddison-Greenwell with Chico, working towards the pesade in-hand. In the finished article, there will be more flexion of the hind legs, and the horse's body will be at a lesser angle to the ground.

A pesade under saddle.

The Leaps

These are the capriole, ballotade, croupade and courbette. The capriole, ballotade and croupade start from the same position but the nature of the leaps varies.

The capriole is probably the best recognized of the leaps; the horse jumps into the air and when he is in the air and his back is virtually horizontal, he kicks out behind. It is said that this movement was developed for the battlefield where the kick would fend off infantry approaching from behind. As this movement puts the horse at the level of a man's head, you can see how effective this might be. The Cadre Noir of Saumur in France has a movement that would have a similar outcome, but the horse's head goes down between his forelegs and the horse purely kicks back with both hind legs.

The ballotade is a similar leap to the capriole, but the hind legs are held in once the horse is off the ground, and the hooves face down.

The croupade is, again, the same leap only with the bottom of the hooves showing from behind.

The courbette is quite different. With this leap the horse lifts the forelegs together off the ground until almost vertical and then jumps off the hind legs, which must also remain together. If a single courbette is ridden, the horse's forelegs will return to the ground after just one jump, but I have seen Alvaro Domecq perform as many as seven successive courbettes in the Royal Andalusian School of Equestrian Art. In November 2005 I am sure that I counted thirteen leaps; the rider being ably assisted from the ground by a trainer.

Each of the above leaps is developed from the piaffe to get the forehand off the ground. So, in order to do these movements, you must first have a good, well-established piaffe to both develop the movement and to return to when things go wrong, as they often do. The croupade, ballotade and capriole need a facility to build up the energy for the leaps. The rider often begins with piaffe, speeds the piaffe up, then turns the movement from one utilizing the clear opposite diagonals of the piaffe into the terre-à-terre (earth to earth), which is a movement where the front and back legs stay almost together in pairs as the horse appears to bounce from front to back until he is able to explode upwards with enough velocity to level out.

These airs above the ground can be, and often are, demonstrated in-hand, with one trainer, or a pair of trainers, working from the ground to establish the same movements. In-hand work is yet another aspect of training that is an art on its own.

With all of these extreme airs, the need for the ultimate control is as obvious as the correct training is imperative; any of the leaps would surely unseat the average rider and, like the levade and pesade, would soon get out of hand if attempted before discipline and gymnastic development were confirmed. You only have to watch any of these movements in slow motion to understand the strength required and the sheer concussion put upon the horse's and the rider's body.

When competition dressage began in the early years of the twentieth century, and greater extension in the gaits was expected in the tests, the Anglo-Arab and the Thoroughbred were the horses of the moment; later in the century, the Hanoverian, Dutch, Danish and Swedish Warmbloods rose in popularity. Because of this it was easy to forget that the Spanish horse had dominated the manège for centuries and was at the birth of dressage as an art form.

Today, the Spanish horse's qualities are again being recognized in the international dressage arena. Their introduction and performances in the Olympics in Atlanta (1996) astounded many because they had such high placings in both the team and individual dressage events; and they performed with such aplomb. We have Ignacio Ramblas and the Pure-bred Spanish stallion Evento to thank for this. Together, they gave the Spanish horse a huge boost in the competition-dressage market-place. Now Rafael Soto carries on the good work with the very baroque-type stallion Invasor, whose work in collection always gains him such good marks, which more than makes up for his lack of extension in walk and trot. This is the opposite image to that presented by many Warmbloods, who tend to extend with great expression but struggle in piaffe.

Perhaps now a little of the finesse and beauty of the *doma clasica* will find its way into the competition arena, and the Spanish horse can once again become number one in the manège.

Chapter Five

About the Spanish Horse

THE SPANISH HORSE HAS evolved, with some help from mankind, into a breed with a number of different types within the breed. This has been dictated by the purpose for which serious breeders intend to use the horse and what market-place it is intended to fill.

Whilst the Spanish horse's purpose may have changed over the centuries, the breed's excellent characteristics (proven historically to have been of such great value) have been retained because the Spanish horse has the strongest of genes; why else would the equestrian world be built to such a great degree upon his blood? It has given presence, stamina, temperament, agility, courage and beauty to so many breeds.

There are, however, those breeders who may go about their business in a somewhat haphazard way, and I fear that, without a good knowledge of riding and training, they are breeding purely from show-ring success, and believe they can establish a stud in a few years on the back of this. This is particularly the case outside Spain where the gene pool is smaller and there are fewer horses to compare with, and choose from, and perhaps the expertise and knowledge are not so readily available.

People also appear to believe that breeding by putting two champions together is a foolproof method of obtaining future winners for any field; but there are no short cuts, it takes a lifetime to develop a good breeding pro-gramme that has consistency of type and reliability of temperament and that has not been spoilt by in-breeding too closely.

Breeding is not easy; it takes investment, inspiration, hard work, patience and a certain amount of luck. (The careful choice of the right foundation mares and suitable stallions does at least reduce the degree of chance in a breeding programme, but an element always remains.) Then there is the careful management of each animal's vital early years, in particular the feeding and rearing programme. It is most important that the youngstock are turned out in groups as they grow so that they can play and learn together.

A horse may have been bred to look good, but the next important question is, when it comes to work, does he? The better studs in Spain and Portugal are realizing the benefit of employing experienced trainers to assist with the training of all their horses. Some of the famous Spanish studs and breeders are: Bohorquez Escriband Candou, Cardenas, Domecq, Jose Luis Escalera and Maria Escalera.

With good feedback from trainers, adjustments can be made to breeding programmes in accordance with what is discovered during training. In addition to this, a well-presented stallion in the show classes is a good advertisement for the stud. These classes now include a ridden section which is essential to the overall points when judging a breeding stallion; it is no longer just a case of morphology and movement (*morfologia y movimiento*).

There are also those studs that have for many years nurtured a dream of producing a horse of good quality and type, with a purpose; this may be bullfighting, dressage or driving, and each purpose has different requirements. This in itself is fine if high breeding standards are maintained, but not everyone will necessarily agree with the type produced. For example, in the case of competition dressage it would appear that many breeders worldwide (including Spain) have aimed to produce, again with the market in mind, a bigger, sport-horse type of Spanish horse of 16.2 hh or over, when for many years the usual height was less than 15.2 hh. As a consequence, in the last two decades, many Spanish horses have started to look more like Warmbloods and are, in my opinion, moving away from the correct type.

If you study the paintings by Velasquez, drawings from the Duke of Newcastle's time and many sculptures in major cities around Europe, for example, and look at the horse in proportion to the rider, you will see that the rider's leg comes well below the barrel of his mount, and his shoulders well above the horse's ears. Even bearing in mind that mankind's average height has increased since the medieval period, it is quite obvious that the Spanish horses of the period were not tall.

We should be grateful, therefore, that some breeders are still breeding the old *Cartujano* type – so lovingly nurtured by the Carthusian monks for centuries – so that we can go back to these lines for excellent Spanish attributes. The famous Terry horses, which carry the Bocao brand, are Carthusian, and the Terry line is present in many well-known Spanish family trees.

No matter how often we deviate from the classical type of Spanish horse, we can, at least, still return to the wonderful characteristics of the Carthusian.

The Spanish horse is the most aesthetically pleasing of horses. The breed's qualities include without doubt: presence, movement, agility, grace, courage and, above all, a temperament that exceeds all others. We shall look at a number of the Spanish horse's facets in this chapter and shall begin with how the names of the different types were acquired.

The well-known Spanish stallion, Oficial, owned by Maria Jose Ruiz Fernandez of Yeguada Susaeta, is renowned for both his beauty and his extravagant movement.

What's in a Name?

The Spanish Pure-bred

Andalusia, the fascinating and exhilarating area of Southern Spain (see Chapter 2), gave its name to the horse it has nurtured for centuries: the Andalusian. The predominance of Spanish horse breeding remains in Andalusia today, possibly owing to the richness of the soil and abundance of good water from the Andalusian mountains, or perhaps because of the area's strong links to the riding culture itself.

The official name 'Andalusian' was, however, changed in 1912, when the *Spanish State Stud Book* was formed. The Spanish horse had been referred to as the Andalusian for so long, many of the breeders wanted the name to remain, but it was not to be. I am sure that for reasons of commercialism and fairness to breeders of Spanish horses all over Spain and, indeed, the world, it was only right that the new official name for the Andalusian became the Pura Raza Española (PRE), the Spanish Pure-bred; a name that, by its nature, makes it easy to use the term 'Spanish horse'. But I am convinced that, officialdom notwithstanding, people will continue to call this breed the Andalusian.

Coincidentally, at about this time competition dressage came to prominence in Europe. And how strange that the Andalusian, once believed to be the greatest horse in the world, the one horse that stood at the very roots of equitation itself and on whose back nearly all we know of classical horsemanship was discovered, should also lose favour in the competition-dressage arena at this time. This exclusion lasted for very nearly 100 years, until the Atlanta Olympics when the Spanish re-presented their horses to the competition world and did so well.

Sometimes the pure-bred Spanish horse is known as the Spanish Thoroughbred, and the Spanish themselves often promote the horse outside Spain with this name. I feel this is unnecessary and confusing because many may be led to believe that they are referring to a Thoroughbred bred in Spain.

The term 'Iberian horse' is occasionally used but, strictly, this term should also cover all the other breeds and types of the whole Iberian Peninsula, which includes Portugal.

This I hope demonstrates the difficulties and misunderstandings that come about when facts are lost in translation, or through inaccurate information.

Two young Spanish Pure-breds: LEFT *Pasodoble as a young colt.* BELOW *Farolero at three-and-a-half.*

ABOVE *Farolero in action.*

Destinado, who was owned by Debbie Leng and Roger Taylor (of Queen fame).

Part-breds

As well as the pure-bred horse, there are a number of Spanish cross-breds favoured by the Spanish for particular jobs. They are the Hispano Arabe (*Arabe*, not Arab, if you want to refer to the breed in the Spanish way), the Tres Sangres, the Spanish/Thoroughbred and Spanish/Lusitano crosses, and the Cruzado.

HISPANO ARABE

The Hispano Arabe is, as the name suggests, a cross between a pure-bred Spanish horse and a pure-bred Arab.

In Spain it is more common to put an Arab stallion to a Spanish mare. This has, over the years, been proven to produce a wonderful horse with all the good points of each breed: the temperament, power, agility, elevation in the gaits and movements from the Spanish blood, and the speed, stamina and straightness in movement of the Arab. Both horses can possess great courage and presence. Whilst an experienced eye can tell an Hispano Arabe just by observing the characteristics from both these breeds, it is well to remember that, like many crosses, they can come in many and varied packages; particularly as an Hispano Arabe can have differing percentages of blood from each side. For example, a pure-bred Spanish stallion put to an Hispano Arabe mare should, obviously, produce a horse more Spanish- than Arab-looking, and so on.

As stated, the Arab stallion/Spanish mare cross produces the best results with the most consistency, but the reverse cross is also carried out. Either of these crosses between two pure-breds is called a first cross and will inevitably contain 50% of the blood of each breed. Hispano Arabes can also be crossed with each other and Hispano Arabes can be crossed with pure-bred Spanish horses: all these crosses produce Hispano Arabes with various percentages of Spanish blood but, to be considered an Hispano Arabe, a horse must contain a minimum of 25% Spanish blood.

When a Spanish stallion is used in the mating he must be fully graded (see Chapter 6). Similarly, any Hispano Arabe must be graded for the progeny to enter the *Spanish State Stud Book*.

The Arab is a very popular breed in Spain, where there are many top-quality Arabs; the breeding classes are well attended and, overall, highly regarded. Sadly, in Britain and other countries, this is not always the case. Whilst the Arab has been extremely popular in Britain for many years this has, to some degree, been the breed's downfall. Although there are some very fine

Peter Maddison-Greenwell with the garrocha *at Broadgate Arena on the Hispano Arabe, Chico, bred by Jenny Bernard. Chico was one of the first horses involved in El Caballo de España. Dancing in the background is El Moreno, a great flamenco dancer and a great friend.*

examples of this impressive breed in Britain, too many poor-quality Arabs have been bred, usually because amateur owners have mares who for one reason or another, cannot jump, do dressage, are of poor conformation for showing, and, in so many cases, are of dubious character and thus unpleasant to ride and handle. So what do these owners do? They breed from them, thus perpetuating the problem. And this is not the prerogative of Arab breeding; unfortunately it will happen in any breed.

Spanish horses are still a rare breed in Britain and are, on the whole, of good quality, but if you put a poor Arab specimen to a good Spanish stallion it is very unlikely that a good Hispano Arabe would be produced; there have to be genes of good quality on both sides.

In Spain the Hispano-Arabe plays a very important role in both the bull-ring and out in the country. This cross-breed's superior speed makes it a favourite for the first part of a mounted bullfight, when the bull is still fresh; and its versatility and ability to endure a hard day's work makes it popular amongst the *vaquera* riders for both work and competition.

TRES SANGRES

Unlike the Hispano Arabe, the Tres Sangres does not have an official register and so there is no grading nor any directives and these horses do not achieve *Spanish State Stud Book* status. Nevertheless, this is a highly prized cross and is also extremely popular with *vaquera* riders and *rejoneodors*.

Tres Sangres means Three Bloods and they are Spanish, Arab and Thoroughbred. As you can imagine with the three hottest of bloods flowing through his veins this horse can be supercharged and not for the faint-hearted. But take this abundance of energy and enhance it with tact and experience and you have at your fingertips a creature of beauty who can float through the air with more than a touch of Allah's breath.

For me, the ideal Tres Sangres combination is an Anglo-Arab mare put to a Pure-bred Spanish stallion, which should result in a short-coupled, big-moving horse with a roundness of neck and quarters that balances both ends. The head should be small with big, expressive eyes and small ears, and the tail low set and full. Again, the Spanish elevation meets the Arab stride-length, and all is encased in a skin of shot silk.

SPANISH/THOROUGHBRED CROSS

Like the Tres Sangres, this horse does not have an official status but is an excellent cross when both parents are well selected. Good selection is important because, for some reason, this same cross can come out with the worst elements of both breeds rather than the best, in the same way that Shire Horse/Thoroughbred crosses can be amazing or a disaster. My feelings are that, as with some of the British Spanish/Arab crosses, this is because of poor judgement in the selection of the mare to be put to the Spanish stallion.

Having said this, however, I have seen many successful Spanish/Thoroughbred crosses, and have a super chap in my yard who possesses a beauty and charm matched only by his endless energy. He has the ability to perform all

aspects of *vaquera* and *clasica* work and takes to new challenges with a lust for learning and an immense leap of faith – sometimes literally!

Saeta, a Tres Sangres stallion, on the move.

SPANISH/LUSITANO CROSS

This is simply a cross of the best bloodlines of the Spanish and Lusitano breeds. It may be a particularly beneficial cross if a Spanish horse whose off-spring are destined for the bullring is crossed with a Lusitano line famed for its ability in this field.

CRUZADO

This is the official name given to any other cross that possesses Spanish blood, and this is what will appear on your cross-bred's papers. When the parentage of the non-Spanish horse cannot be established, *indefinida* (indefinite) will appear on the papers.

Warmbloods, Welsh Cobs and Connemaras have produced some excellent horses when crossed with Spanish stallions. The result of the cross between the Quarter Horse and the Spanish is the Azteca; according to Dr Deb Bennet in her book *Conquerors The Roots of New World Horsemanship*:

The mare Diamonds For A Lifetime is by the famous Irish Draught stallion, King of Diamonds, out of a Thoroughbred mare. She was put to a Pure-bred Spanish stallion to produce a foal (pictured) who is 50% Spanish, 25% Irish Draught and 25% Thoroughbred.

'An important aspect of Azteca breeding is the pre-planned and systematic crossing of horses who are themselves crossbreds.'

I have bred a number of horses from a particularly good Irish Draught/Thoroughbred mare who is by the famous Irish Draught stallion King of Diamonds. She is a handsome, strong animal with the stamina to hunt all day and the ability to jump a five-bar gate from a standstill, as well as being able to perform the most cadenced and slow pirouettes.

MULES

We cannot really discuss Spanish cross-breds without mentioning the mule. For many centuries, Spanish jack donkeys have sired mules at home for agricultural, pack and draught work, and have been exported all over the world to sire mules for military and freight use. Spanish jacks are quite tall, well conformed but not heavy and, with a carefully chosen mare, can sire tall, elegant and 'handsome' mules; all traits that can be enhanced by Spanish blood. I saw some outstanding examples in Almeria, including one with a beautiful spotted coat. Mules are renowned for their stamina, and today's riding mules are found in just about every equestrian field, to a greater or lesser degree, in a number of countries around the world: endurance, trekking, driving, showing, showjumping, Western, mule racing and dressage.

Conformation

There is an acceptable variation of type in the Spanish horse; for example, the horses favoured for driving might be somewhat stockier than saddle horses, and there may be a specific influence from a particular bloodline. However, as with all breeds, there are certain points of conformation that are recognized as typical requirements. These, as defined in Juan Llamas' book *This is the Spanish Horse*, are:

Head In proportion to body size; sub-convex profile; broad forehead; well set on to the neck with an unobstructed throat to enable good flexion.

Eyes and ears The eyes should be large, dark and almond or triangular shaped; ears should not be too close together, too long or too short.

Neck Has to act as a good balancing agent; arched; high; well set on to shoulder; crest should not be excessively heavy; mane should be long, thick and of a silky texture.

Withers Well defined; not too narrow or too low.

A *champion Spanish stallion.*

Jenny Goodhall's Pure-bred stallion, Fetishe (affectionately known as Freddy) has been both ridden and in-hand champion at The British Association for the Purebred Spanish Horse National Breed Show a number of times, and has been a great ambassador for the breed in the UK.

BELOW Freddy at liberty.

Shoulder Long and sloping (in proportion to horse).

Chest Broad and deep.

Forelegs Strong and clean with good bone; well-muscled forearm; broad knees; cannons tend to be long in the Spanish horse; pasterns of medium slope and length; light feathering.

Back Short and strong; straight; horizontal; well-sprung ribs. (See also Chapter 9.)

Loins Well muscled; broad; strong; rounded.

Croup Gently sloping (angle of about 30 degrees); moderately wide. The tail follows the slope of the croup and, like the mane, is thick, silky and long.

Hind Legs Strong and clean with good bone; well-muscled thigh; broad, strong and springy hocks. Cannons: as for the forelegs; pasterns: as for the forelegs but with a slightly greater angle to the slope; light feathering.

Hooves Small and hard.

The overall picture should be one of an elegant, strong, well-rounded, but not overtly solid or heavy horse, with an air of nobility; and, given the redoubtable ancestry, a touch of arrogance could be said to be acceptable.

The most obvious and distinct conformation trait of the Spanish horse is dishing, something that has been bred in and out of the breed for centuries. There was a time when this was fashionable and in fact quite desired. A fiesta horse or a carriage horse in the past was often known to have 'campañero', a movement when the legs appear to move in an outwardly circular motion from the shoulders. Even dishing from below the knee is frowned upon in competition dressage, no matter how insignificant it is, although I know of no rule that says this should be penalized, provided the horse himself is straight.

A common problem with some Spanish horses is a weak back, which gives the horse a faulty top line: a line from the high head carriage flows over a large crested neck down to the withers from where the back drops down below, and back up to, the quarters, like a radio wave. This may be aesthetically attractive to the uninitiated but, to function well, a riding horse must have the capacity and strength to lift his back like a bridge and carry a rider. A weak back may take years to strengthen systematically, and to get the horse to lower the neck in the early years to improve this can prove problematical.

The beautiful head of a Pure-bred Spanish stallion, Pasodoble.

BELOW *The Tres Sangres stallion, Saeta – alert eye, full nostrils, flowing action.*

Maturity and Temperament

It is important to understand that Spanish and Lusitano horses do not mature as early as most other breeds. Whilst it is often acceptable to begin training a horse at three, if he is ready, I always advocate patience in the work in the first year, with no pushing or pressurizing too soon. This pays in the long run because some of these horses do not finish growing until they are eight years old and, in my experience, stallions can, with good training, develop dramatically between six and ten years of age.

Part-breds may mature more quickly depending on the cross. Since Arabs are also late developers the Hispano Arabe will also mature late. Some horses appear to grow quickly with good food, but do not think that, because your horse is tall and round, he is mature. Hard work at too young an age will damage bones and muscles beyond repair and a horse's life can be over before training has really begun. Just look at the average racing life of a Thorough-bred.

Good temperament is an attribute of the Spanish horse. At major events, large groups of mares often spend much time in peaceful close proximity. The mare in this photograph is wearing a traditional bell.

Good temperament is one of the Spanish breed's most praised and prized possessions, but a considerate attitude to the maturity and training of a horse could help to maintain that temperament. I have handled and trained many Spanish stallions over the last twenty years and can honestly say that they have astounded me time and time again with their forgiving nature. It is very rare to find any well-educated Spanish horse who kicks or bites or has any desire to harm mankind, other horses or even other stallions, and on the whole I have found these horses to be social, even-tempered, willing to please and even loving. I have trusted my horses with many inexperienced grooms and students and they have never let me down.

Nevertheless, I say 'well-educated' advisedly because, sadly, any horse can be spoilt by ignorance and bad handling, and the potential for any stallion to be unpredictable must not be ignored. There are, of course, exceptions to the generality; not every Spanish horse is a 'pussycat'. They need to be, as the Duke of Newcastle said, 'well chosen'. If you have the foundation of a good temperament, then good manners will be easy to instil during the training of a young horse (see Chapter 9).

Something that so many people forget, ignore, or just don't know, is that the Spanish horse is hot-blooded and has evolved to operate with energy in the hot Spanish climate. He may be relatively subdued and obedient when viewed in the heat of the afternoon sun – just think how you feel in intense heat – but when shipped to colder climes, fed a hunter's portion of high-quality, protein-rich feed, or lush grass, and not exercised enough, the energy overload may prove to be highly explosive in a Spanish horse. Many horses have been labelled as unmanageable or having a dangerous temperament because all this has not been taken into account, when it was not the horse, but his management that was at fault (see Chapter 6).

I would like to relate two tales: the first underlines the Spanish horse's good temperament, and the second shows how no horse's temperament should be taken for granted.

Jane Rabagliati, a great and knowledgeable friend of mine, who translated Juan Llamas' book, *This is the Spanish Horse*, has a very personal way of testing a Spanish stallion's amenability; she will, without any prior knowledge of a particular stallion, walk quietly up behind him, put her hand between his hind legs, and gently but firmly holds his *cojónes* (testicles), and the fact that this intrusion is accepted is most certainly an indication of any stallion's tolerant temperament! Remember, Jane knows and understands Spanish horses, and one experienced woman's method may be another person's downfall; *do not try this with any stallion.*

Some years ago the Spanish Riding School was performing in Munich. The 'leapers' entered the arena and after Arthur Kottas's immaculate performance, all eyes were suddenly drawn towards a horse who was supposed to be performing a courbette; but, for that performance, courbette was not on his agenda at all. He was pulling in a way few people will experience, he stood up on his back end, stuck his nose in the air, jumped ten feet forward whilst vertical, then plummeted to the ground with the force of an elephant falling out of a tree. The poor rider was mortified; obviously it was a bad-courbette day for the horse – and we all have them – but his general temperament was not necessarily to blame. Despite the trepidation with which the rider later entered the arena with another horse for his solo performance, this was exemplary, and with each faultless step the rider's smile grew and grew.

Chapter Six

Management of the Spanish Horse

Buying a Spanish Horse

Over the years I have imported a considerable number of horses but, as I have never considered myself a dealer or felt a need to sell horses for the sole purpose of making a living, I can afford the luxury of ensuring that the right horse is matched with the right owner. I am also in the enviable position of being able to say 'no' to people if I feel horse and prospective buyer are not right for each other; and I have seen far too often what can go wrong when horse and buyer are mismatched.

There are always plenty of dealers, in Spain as everywhere else, who will 'do you a deal'; 'do you' being the operative expression. Your first feeling about someone is often the right one; if you don't feel comfortable with a person, for whatever reason, go somewhere else. The secret is to find the right help, and trust that you can negotiate a good, business-like deal; one where all parties walk away happy. An honest dealer will put a fairly realistic price on a horse. If a horse is worth a particular amount, try to negotiate to a certain extent by all means, but don't push your luck and try to get him too cheaply. We all have to eat!

You have two basic options when buying a Spanish horse: buying one in your own country who has either been imported already, or bred here, or importing one directly from Spain. There are a number of buying factors to be considered and I will run through these first. Many of the factors apply to horse purchase generally, but it is those applying particularly to purchasing from Spain that have been detailed; they would also apply to Portugal.

You may choose to follow the buying process through on your own but with advice from an experienced person, or you may choose to employ an agent. If you go down the first road because you feel it might be cheaper, make sure the advice you receive is sound; if things don't go exactly to plan, you may end up with more expense than you budgeted for, or just a lot of disappointment because you didn't get the horse you thought you were buying. A reputable agent is going to be more expensive but if you budget for this, they could save you extra expense in the long run, and you can leave everything up to them.

Buying Factors

Horses for courses

When looking for a suitable Spanish horse there are a number of things to think about. You must be honest about your own riding ability, temperament, capabilities, experience and knowledge; the purpose for which you require the horse and the extent of your budget. Then decide on what would suit you best, and what gender and colour you would prefer. Perfection does not exist – on your side or the horse's – and so you have to be realistic and choose the most suitable partner you can. If the horse has a temperament compatible with yours, that is a good first step.

It is also extremely important to look at the other qualities required of a horse in any chosen equestrian field. A horse bred for bullfighting is not going to be for the nervous pleasure rider; and a kind, even-natured, steady gentleman is not what you want to be mounted on if you are destined for the *rejoneador*'s life. Similarly, a horse with any number of conformation faults will not get the budding dressage star far, and the one with the ideal temperament but an unsightly scar will not do well in the show ring.

Breeding aside, the choice of your horse's gender must be given some serious thought. Many Spanish male horses are kept entire and there will be more stallions than geldings available, indeed it is extremely hard to get a good gelding; if a stallion is gelded in Spain it has usually been done for serious reasons, such as a dangerous vice or unpredictable temperament. But, you still have to ask yourself if a stallion is really what you want. Despite the normally good temperament of these horses (see Chapter 5), stallions still come with particular management requirements. If you have never handled a stallion before, would you be confident about doing so, either when he is on his own or in mixed company? Would you be keeping him at home or in a livery yard? If the latter, would the proprietors be prepared to take a stallion, and would they have the facilities to keep him? Look into all these things before you make a final decision. On the other hand, should you prefer a mare, these specific considerations do not arise, but a couple of broadly similar ones might: some mares can be touchy or sensitive at certain times, and need diplomatic riding and management – which not all riders seem capable of.

Finally, if you are going to train the horse yourself, you must decide whether you want a horse who will make the job as easy as possible for you, or whether you prefer, and are capable of dealing with, a challenge. Nuno Oliviera, one of the most academically knowledgeable trainers of the last hundred years, famous for training many Lusitano and Spanish horses, is said to have become bored with easy horses and, in his later years, sought more difficult challenges – but this may not be your idea of fun.

If you are in any doubt about which Spanish horse might be right for your course, expert advice will make life much easier and happier for both you and the horse; and don't be embarrassed to ask a knowledgeable person you know and trust to accompany you when looking at possible purchases.

When all these important decisions have been made, put out some feelers about Spanish horses for sale and make some appointments to view. But remember, be considerate. Do not waste people's time if, deep down, you feel a particular horse is not for you. There is certainly no need to ride a horse if you have already decided against purchase, in fact the owner will respect you for this. It takes time to prepare a horse for prospective buyers and the less he is ridden by strangers, the better.

ASSESSMENT PROCEDURE

Observe the horse in the stable being tied up, groomed, tacked up and led out. Study his general stable manners and look for signs of nervousness, crib-biting, weaving, or any other vice. If a horse has a vice but is ideal for you in all other respects, then you might still choose to take the horse on if you have the understanding and skill to deal with the vice. This is a choice you must make with care.

Ask the owner or trainer to show you what the horse can do and, if you like what you see thus far, ask if you (or your allocated rider) can ride him. Be careful: you do not know the horse and he does not know you. Be patient: take a little time to work in walk in order to get a feel for his temperament as well as his movement and ability, and give clear aids when you ask him to do something.

It is important to find out how good the horse is in traffic. If you are buying a horse in Spain remember that, if he has led his life in the country, it is probable that he will have come across far less traffic than a horse living in, say, Britain. Similarly, he may never have travelled; find out if he loads and, if so, whether he will load in both a trailer and a horsebox. This is a big consideration because, if his first journey – let alone his first long journey – is to be to another country from Spain, then you must be aware of the problems this might present. These problems are not necessarily insurmountable, but at least you will know what you are dealing with and you can, if necessary, take advice on making the whole experience as easy for him as possible.

Price

If you are happy with everything you have seen, heard and experienced, and have decided to buy, now is the time to get down to business. Confirm the asking price and then see if there is any room for negotiation. Many people put a little on the price in order to give the impression they are helping you out by dropping it, but others will not negotiate; the price is the price. Pricing can be difficult and you might have to acknowledge that a horse is *worth* more than you can afford; but if you were honest about your budget, the seller should not have shown you a horse out of your price league in the first place, and you should not be too shocked by the price.

Vetting and insurance

Once the price is agreed, I prefer to have the basic details confirmed in writing (i.e. price agreed, any deposit paid, description of horse, etc.) subject to a vet's findings. There are good vets in Spain; if you can't get one recommended, visit some surgeries and discuss the requirements with them. If you are insuring the horse, the insurers may require a specific standard of vetting to be carried out which, depending on the horse's value, may include X-rays; get your insurance company to tell you exactly what they will require. (It is advisable to find out all about the insurance before you start looking because this could be a major purchase and full insurance could be costly.) If the horse is travelling from Spain, you should also consider the risks of transportation, and insure the horse from the date of purchase in Spain.

As far as transportation is concerned, it is advisable to contact some professional horse transporters with good reputations who can take care of the complete job for you. They understand the paperwork, passports, customs requirements, etc.

If the horse's new home is to be in the USA, there are specific points the vetting must include. A blood sample will be taken, which will be checked in laboratories in both Spain and the USA for signs of piroplasmosis (also known as equine malaria or Texas fever, amongst other titles). The horse will also be checked for dourine (a sexually transmitted disease), glanders and equine infectious anaemia. If mares and stallions over two years of age have been used for breeding, they must also be monitored for contagious equine metritis (CEM), a highly contagious bacterial venereal disease, which will involve a quarantine period of about three weeks in Spain prior to export (see Importation below). Horses younger than two years, and geldings, are exempt from this quarantine, as are (since July 2003) mares and stallions who can be proved not to have been used for breeding.

Once you have been advised of the vet's findings and, hopefully, been given some sound advice, the choice of how you act on those findings is, again, yours. Depending on the intended use of the horse, certain flaws may not affect your choice. For example, a breeding stallion who is reasonably priced because of an injury that would impede his movement for dressage, but which would not prevent him from doing his main job, would be well worth the money if breeding is all you require of him.

Payment

Ideally, buyers are well advised not to part with all their hard-earned money before the horse is safely in the horsebox. This is possible if cash is being paid and the buyer picks up the horse in person. A vendor would be equally wise not to let the horse out of sight until the cash has changed hands, or the money is confirmed to be safely in the bank account. When a cheque is involved, trust and patience are required on both sides.

Trust becomes a major issue if you are buying abroad because you almost always have to send your money via the banks to an intermediary or direct to the owner before they will release the horse for transportation. In this case, I am afraid it is the purchaser who must do the trusting, which is all the more reason for researching the vendors and/or getting good recommendations from previous clients, plus information on how straightforward the arrangements were for them.

Important papers

When you are buying Spanish or Lusitano horses, whether they are pure-bred or part-bred, they should have papers. These are issued by the prospective governing bodies. Identification marks are recorded on the papers, but the techniques have changed over the years. At one time all Spanish pure-bred horses were tattooed on the bottom lip as well as sporting their breeder's brand: stallions were branded on the nearside of the hindquarters, and mares on the offside. This was usually done in their first year. Some Spanish horses may have an X branded on a shoulder; this came about during the period of the dangerous African virus (pestiquina) that was a great problem during the 1980s and 1990s. The only other brand a Spanish horse might carry is a breeder's number. Both these last two brands are found very rarely. Nowadays the horses are microchipped; the tiny chip is injected under the skin and can be read by a scanner.

All these details can be checked out before you purchase the horse. Simply ask to have a copy of the papers and get these verified by the particular association's registrar. To speed up the process even more, you could ask the association to do everything for you, but you must be prepared to pay for the service, which is well worth doing because it can save you a lot of problems later. For example, it has been known for unpapered horses to be sold with a dead horse's papers, or for important details to have been Tippexed out of the original papers (of which you may have seen only a copy), etc. For the association's registrar to then find the horse's correct papers is a much harder job, entailing more expense for you. If you only want a horse for hacking and general pleasure riding, having an unpapered horse is not a problem, but the correct papers are essential if you want to breed or compete (or both) with the horse.

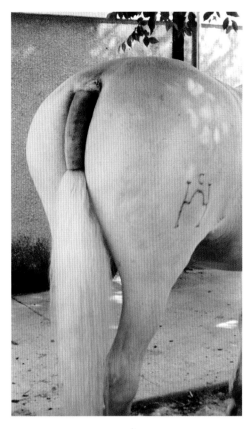

A *Spanish mare clearly branded on the offside flank. She also has a shaved tail, typical of a mare used for breeding.*

IMPORTATION

Importing a horse to Britain is a relatively simple operation. A Spanish state vet must inspect the horse within the forty-eight hours prior to travel. If the horse is found to be infection free, the vet will stamp the transportation papers and the horse is free to travel. There will be no quarantine required on arrival in Britain. Even if the horse is papered, the purchaser will still have to acquire a correct equine passport, as now required by British law, when the horse arrives on British soil.

Importing a Spanish-bred horse into the USA, on the other hand, is a more strictly controlled process. All horses will have to undergo three days of quarantine at the airport on arrival in the USA. In addition to this, the horse is required to be quarantined for contagious equine metritis in Spain prior to travel (see Vetting and Insurance) and must also undergo a period of

CEM quarantine at a US state-approved quarantine station: stallions for one month, mares for two weeks.

The legal and veterinary requirements for travelling horses could be changed at any time; do your homework and make sure every detail is covered. As stated, a professional transporter will probably be the best option and less traumatic (even though it may be more expensive) than organizing the transportation yourself.

To Breed or not to Breed?

When buying a Spanish horse, there are, as mentioned, many aspects to be considered; what size, gender and colour and, most importantly, what is the horse wanted for?

Here I would like to discuss, not so much the actual process of breeding, but more what you need to consider when buying your horse if breeding is a relevant factor.

When discussing a prospective purchase, the first question I ask the buyer is: 'What do you want to do with the horse, and is it likely that you will want to breed from this mare/stallion at some stage?' If the answer is 'yes', then, in addition to their papers, horses must be graded before their progeny can be entered into the *Spanish State Stud Book*. The grading is an approval for breeding by the Jefatura de Cría Caballar of the Spanish Ministry of Defence, and constitutes an important part of the horse's value.

Bear in mind that, when you buy a youngster, the animal's potential is not a guarantee of grading. However, if the horse is intended just for riding or driving and you do not want to breed, the requirements are somewhat different. There are many excellent pure-bred papered horses who may not have passed their grading, or may not even have been submitted for grading, and it might not be too late to get them graded should you decide to do so. The value of ungraded horses, therefore, is not based on their breeding potential but on their suitability for a particular purpose. You must be aware of this when you buy a horse; it is no good thinking you only require a riding horse, then years later being unhappy about not being able to retire the horse to stud because he had failed his grading before you bought him.

Do not expect to pay a moderate amount for a mature Spanish Pure-bred graded stallion who can also compete seriously in Prix St Georges dressage. At the other extreme, you might just find an unpapered horse with some Spanish blood who is capable of good work, for a modest price.

At the time of purchase, it is important to bear in mind what the various categories imply:

Graded means that a horse is graded for breeding, but you must have the correct papers as proof of this.

Papered means that a horse should be exactly as described on the papers.

An **unpapered** horse means that you get what you see and nothing more.

The Jefatura de Cría Caballar are in control of all Spanish breeding documentation worldwide and hold the *Spanish State Stud Book*. In Spain there are officials in each area who will visit and grade a horse who has been first registered as a Spanish Pure-bred; to qualify for registration, both parents must be approved for breeding. There are no exceptions. Countries outside Spain are visited by a grading party that should comprise a vet, a breeder and an army official from the Jefatura de Cría Caballar.

A horse submitted for grading will be measured to establish height, width (which is measured from shoulder to shoulder, usually with a large calliper), bone, etc; and all the Spanish characteristics will be checked: eyes, ears, set of tail, etc. The horse will then be assessed as to suitability for entry into the *Spanish State Stud Book*.

A horse may not pass the grading for many reasons; something as obvious as a fallen crest or as subtle as a high-set tail may influence the decision. Whatever the outcome, it is to be hoped that, with the right training, a horse will still become a good working horse; not every horse is, or should be, destined for reproduction.

Pastures New

Acclimatizing a Spanish-bred horse to new environments and conditions may take time, thought and patience, and the first step is to acknowledge and understand that the animal's Spanish lifestyle might well have been very different from that which he is going to have to get used to in Britain.

Climate

Any Spanish horse coming into Britain from the hot south of Spain will find it harder to acclimatize to the British weather than one from the more temperate north of Spain. Southern Spanish nights can be cold, but it is the damp and wet of the British climate from which a Spanish horse might, initially, need a little protection.

Feeding

In Spain they often feed crushed oats, barley, good straw and alfalfa. The nutritional value of the oats or barley freshly crushed in Spain may be quite different from that of these crops in other countries. You will need, therefore, to introduce new feedstuffs gradually. It would also be worth asking the former Spanish owners to give you a note of exactly what the horse had been fed. Some large studs might even have diet sheets they could give you.

To start with, I tend to give newcomers three small feeds a day to keep the stomach and intestines working. Good hay is a must and can be given at regular intervals. The amount and type of feed you give will depend on the job your new Spanish horse must do. There are many good feed merchants with specialist knowledge who can give you advice and help if you are concerned. The needs of a yearling, a young colt or filly, a mature working or competition horse, or a brood mare or a veteran stallion for stud work, will all be quite different.

Spanish horses are very good doers and do not need to eat the same amount as many of their counterparts. Many can live on very meagre portions, so *do not overfeed* your new horse, especially a ridden one; this can lead to laminitis or, at the very least, an extremely lively horse whom you cannot handle. The quantity of fuel being taken in must not exceed the energy being expended.

GRAZING AND EXERCISE

Grazing is an interesting subject. The British have a tendency to think that every horse wants to graze for at least eight hours a day all through the year, yet Spanish horses are usually kept in all day and just get the occasional spin in the manège, or are lunged, then given a quick hose-down and put back into the stable or stall.

I have found that many of the horses we have had from Spain and Portugal are used to being tied up in stalls or stables for a few days at a time without much work. Whilst not ideal, for general work this has not proved to be detrimental to their temperament or well-being, owing, to a great degree, to their inherent easy-going temperament. I, like many, owing to limited facilities, have for nearly twenty years kept my stallions stabled and stalled all year and have been successful in maintaining good temperaments and manners. This method is, for me, preferable to turning out; the stallions do not injure themselves by galloping over-excitedly round fields and into fences, or over-reaching. The regular, interesting and varied work I give them ensures they remain calm and relaxed. People often say to me that my horses always look happy and stress-free when they work and perform.

If you do wish to graze your stallion, my advice is: get to know him well first and gain his respect, and then gradually introduce him to a small, safe grazing environment. Lush grasses as found in many parts of Britain, the USA and other places will be too rich for him, and so it is important that he is only allowed to graze for a very short time at first. Once he has become accustomed to the grass, in most cases a stallion will only need to go out for a short time each day or perhaps just for a little relaxation every few days, if you choose. You will certainly find most sensible stallions by the gate waiting to be brought back into the warm, dry comfort of their stables, especially in the cold, wet seasons.

You may want brood mares and youngstock to live out in the summer, which they can do after they, like the stallions, have been introduced to the grazing in a sensible manner as just described. Whilst we have only bred a few horses for ourselves, we have kept many for clients and find that keeping mares and youngstock in a barn from, say, October to March, can both save your paddocks and make care easier in the winter months. In this situation they can be fed less but will still maintain condition, which they would lose if they were left out unattended in the worst of winter weather. Although these horses are tough and have historically endured extreme conditions, there is absolutely no reason to put their hardiness to the test.

There is an argument that it is natural for mares to lose weight in the winter as they get pregnant more easily if they are not fat; this may or may not be true but it could hardly be in the mare's or foal's interest for the mare to be actually 'poor' at the time of conception. Either way, there is a big difference between that which nature might dictate and allowing a mare to be under-nourished.

FAT IS NOT FIT

Some breeders like to see their youngstock big, fat and round as early as two years old. To achieve this they pump their horses with fattening foods right from the very beginning. They may believe this gives a horse a good start in life or that, come sale time, when the horse is two or three years old, the fat covers a multitude of conformation problems. But young horses need to be well fed, not overfed. Being overweight causes as many problems for horses as it does for humans, and other animals.

A while ago, a client had bought a stallion through us. He came over from Spain bristling with muscle and was able to perform piaffe and flying changes. When I next saw him, two years later, he was obese and resembled a Suffolk Punch rather than the good Spanish riding horse he was.

The owner was also having considerable problems with his work: he was showing a reluctance to canter, not tracking up, and showing no signs of cadence or elevation. After much observation and discussion we came to the conclusion that this was down to a combination of things including uneducated tuition, the rider's poor seat, and lethargy arising from the stallion's excess weight. The owner had, like so many others, turned her splendid Spanish stallion into a fat old cob. She had not heeded the advice given and turned her horse out at the first opportunity; even through the winter he was out four hours a day. He was huge when I saw him in March, but I dread to think what he would have looked like and what could have happened to him had she continued to turn him out on spring grass. We likened it to a human stuffing himself with sweets until he exploded. I am pleased to say she listened to us, kept her horse's diet in check and continues to visit us with her much improved horse and riding ability.

Shoeing

It is quite hard to find a good farrier in Spain and occasionally you will hear someone admit that they do their own shoeing. Spanish farriers often prefer to work on a horse's feet with someone else holding the foot up for them, as I know to my cost! One of the reasons for this might be that, owing to the dry, rocky terrain they live and work in, many Spanish horses' feet are steely hard. Such feet sometimes have to be cut back with a hammer and hoof knife (conventional hoof cutters won't touch them) and it is probably easier for a farrier who has to work like this to have someone else hold the foot up. An imported Spanish horse's hard hooves are not likely to change, even in a wetter climate, if the horse is kept in the Spanish way, i.e. stabled or stalled for much of the time. A Spanish horse bred in Britain or the USA will have the type of hooves his bloodline and lifestyle have given him.

In Britain it can be hard to find a good farrier who is willing to listen to you and consult you regarding your Spanish horse's feet, which are, and should be, quite different from those of English horses. I have been very lucky in this regard with my farrier of many years, Ashley Tilley, who has shod many of our and our clients' horses with excellent results; not only is he prepared to listen and learn, but he will also accept a second opinion on certain matters.

If you have a good farrier, value, work with, and listen to him; he can literally keep your horse on his feet! A great friend, Dr Giles Holtom PhD, FWCF, has nursed one of our horses through white line disease and sheared heels and he is still in serious work today. On the contrary, if a farrier is not familiar with the structure of the Spanish horse's feet, it is important that he finds out everything he needs to know from someone with the relevant experience.

The Spanish Pure-bred has a tendency towards boxy feet (i.e. feet in which the frog does not contact the ground, the heels are often more closed than open, and the sole may be hollow or curved) to protect the frog, sole and inner sensitive structures against the dry, rocky terrain he has evolved in. The feet are also often allowed to grow very long, particularly the front feet – which might be useful if your horse is lacking a little height when it comes to his grading assessment! Whilst this shape of foot does not give the Spanish horse any problems, whether he is working in rough, mountainous regions or in the *vaquera* and *clasica* arenas, it is not good for the feet of dressage horses such as the Warmbloods, and their feet should not be made boxy by poor shoeing.

The farrier's task is to change the feet if they were previously bad but it is imperative that this is done gradually, over a series of sessions; they must be changed only as much as is necessary for the horse's new environment, and rebalanced accordingly. The farrier should not be tempted to open up the hooves like those of an English hunter; a Spanish horse does not need a big base area over which to stand. If it is necessary to change the type of shoe worn as well (some Spanish horses are still shod with a wide, unfullered shoe) this process should also be gradual.

There are also a number of 'styles' of shoeing which are popular at the moment, 'natural shoeing' or 'barefoot' for example, and whilst I have heard a number of arguments supporting this kind of shoeing, and it might suit certain horses particularly well, I remain unconvinced about it with regard to the majority of hard-working horses. I have never had a problem with good conventional shoes and shoeing for nearly forty years, although our horses nowadays tend to have front shoes only because we have very little roadwork.

¿Habla Inglés?

Will a horse trained in Spain understand English, or any other languages come to that? The answer to this is probably not initially, but recent research shows that horses can recognize and understand some words, and if a horse can do that with the Spanish language, he might take a little while to adapt to English. In many cases, however, it is not the spoken word that instigates a response so much as the tone of voice and the way in which the word is delivered when giving a horse a verbal command. For example, if you give a horse the verbal instruction to 'Can-ter', lifting the voice a little for the second half of the word, is a horse going to differentiate between this and the word 'San-ta' delivered in the same way? No, because he recognizes the sound of the word and the emphasis.

However, recognition of words might be a small problem for a Spanish-trained horse listening to English speech for the first time, particularly if a word does not sound the same as the one he is used to. The few words that we tend to use when lungeing, for example, are: 'walk', 'trot', 'canter' and 'whooooa'. These words in Spanish are: *paso*, *trote*, *galope* and *whooooa*, and so you can see that the Spanish words for 'walk' and 'canter' are very different from the English words, but the Spanish horses will adapt to English far more quickly than we could learn to speak Spanish, I am sure. This process will be hastened, if the horse is old enough to be ridden, by giving the correct aids for a gait simultaneously with the verbal aid.

Language is something that we have never found to be a problem; all our horses appear to be multi-lingual, that is, they can ignore us equally whatever language we use!

With patience, understanding, common sense and the correct balanced approach to feeding, work, discipline and welfare, you will prevent many problems that could make keeping your Spanish horse difficult, or, on very rare occasions, even dangerous, leaving you more time to enjoy the experience of living and working with a Spanish horse.

Chapter Seven

Spanish Tack, Costume and Presentation of the Horse

I
N SPAIN, AS IN BRITAIN and many other countries, all manner of new concepts in tack and riding wear are creeping in to the equestrian world, and this can be confusing for the uninitiated.

All manifestations of tack and equipment are now available, and in the most unlikely materials. It is now possible to deck your horse out in reflective, luminescent, fluorescent, multi-coloured and stitched headcollars, lead ropes, bridles and saddles. Just imagine the embarrassment of the horse who has to wear the latest orange 'ecstatic mouth' rubber bit, hanging from a bright red bridle finished with shiny white plastic edges. To complement this, you can sit on a purple, suede-look, neoprene-surfaced, indestructible plastic saddle designed by the latest computer software, utilizing every technological advance that science can conjure up. Furthermore, your feet can rest in stirrups made from the same heat-resistant plastic, baked to withstand rapid re-entry into the earth's atmosphere and yet light enough to wear as earrings. Why?

Whilst in some fields 'anything goes' is an acceptable attitude, I believe that, in riding, care should be taken to uphold tradition; presentation is not only steeped in tradition but is of paramount importance. The Spanish especially take great pride in the presentation of their horses and themselves.

The traditional Spanish tack and costume play essential roles in this presentation and woe betide anyone who turns up at a competition in the wrong outfit with the wrong tack. Before entering the ring, each horse and rider are scrupulously inspected. As with any English showing class, you must be absolutely correct in every detail if you are to pass muster. The judges will not smile upon anyone who mixes their tack and costumes inappropriately, even if everyone in the class appears to be equally misinformed or oblivious of etiquette. You cannot change things just because you don't like the collar, the trousers make your bum look fat or you would prefer the jacket to have silver sparkly bits on the shoulders. It is simply a case of following tradition and etiquette in a way that does you and your horse credit. This all applies equally to the Portuguese classes (see Chapter 8).

This way of life, art form, sport, or however you see it, takes on the responsibility of honouring its history and the horse on whom it is performed; it does not benefit from tasteless distractions.

For me, correctness is a very important part of Spanish horsemanship; you feel immense pride when saddling up with the correct tack and donning the correct costume. You know you are representing the *jinetes* of the past. Centuries of history and tradition have shaped the tack we use and the costume we wear today, for any competition or show. For it to create that feeling of worth for you and your horse, it must be understood and, furthermore, respected.

Doma Vaquera Tack

Vaquera tack is specific to the country and the ranching life; it is practical and has evolved to do a particular job.

The Saddle (*Silla Vaquera*) and its Accoutrements

The saddle is distinctive and has hardly changed its appearance for centuries. Whoever the manufacturer may be, the basic style is the same, but perhaps with some minor variations.

The *vaquera* saddle, used for both work and competition, is of a totally different construction from the continental dressage saddles we are so familiar with today. It has been said that the original work saddle evolved from early pack saddles. These simple wooden constructions had an X-shaped fork at the front and rear that sat over the horse's back near the withers and quarters respectively to stabilize the structure. This would seem logical when you think that a *vaquera* saddle has a rigid form at the front and back and has a flexible seat, which is made from leather with straw running in stitched bands from front to back. This is supported by a padded area that lies down each shoulder, on either side of the backbone, and spreads out into a half-moon shape that runs at rights angles to and across the backbone, loading the weight evenly and flexibly on a wider area than is usual with the more familiar European saddles.

You sit on a thick sheepskin (*asiento*) seat placed over the saddle seat, which is shaped both in front and behind your legs in much the same way as the 'great saddle' (of the type used by Antoine de Pluvinel) would have been shaped.

The *vaquera* saddle has a high cantle (*concha*) that has the same purpose as those on medieval saddles: to prevent the rider being thrown out the back door.

A few inches back from the front fork, the girth (*cincha*) covers the whole circumference of horse and saddle, like a surcingle. The girth has a large, two-pinned buckle which is stitched into the girth on the nearside at a point where there is a strap facing you that points downwards. The bulk of the girth goes away from you, up, through and over the saddle; it then goes round and under the horse's belly and back up to the strap in front of you. At the end of the girth is a square of metal that this strap goes through before going back up to and through the buckle, where it is pulled down (which should be done with care because it exerts some considerable leverage); the buckle pins are then placed in the holes, which finally secures the girth.

The stirrup leather (*acion de estribo*) starts off as one long length of sturdy leather attached to the stirrup itself, which is taken up to the underside of the stirrup buckle, situated just behind the girth. It is then fed up through the

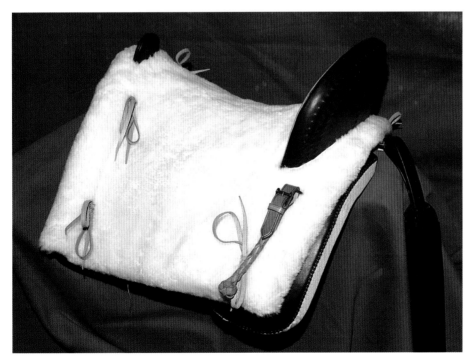

A *typical vaquera saddle.*

77

buckle from behind, drawn towards you, down and through the stirrup, back up again to the buckle and is then pierced by the pin of the buckle securing it in position and fixing its length. The excess leather strap is pushed up and under the sheepskin seat. It is advisable to know the stirrup length you are most comfortable with because there is no easy way to alter the *vaquera* stirrup when mounted. If you change horses frequently with another rider, be prepared for an uncomfortable ride as their leathers might be too short or too long for you.

Once, when doing a display, I had two helpful grooms who kindly offered to alter my leathers whilst I was mounted. The music had started, the introduction had been done and the audience was primed. The grooms rushed to alter one leather apiece, by two holes as requested. Unfortunately, one of them adjusted two holes up and one of them two holes down. *Doma vaquera* at the gallop is exciting enough; I did not need to feel that I was trick-riding as well.

The stirrup (*estribo vaquero*) itself is made of steel (not stainless steel, which is rust-resistant) and coated in a black protective substance formed during the manufacturing process when the steel stirrup is dipped into oil; this does rub off after considerable use, leaving the stirrup liable to rust if it is not kept clean and regularly coated in oil.

The sides of the stirrup are triangular and the whole foot rests on a flat rectangular plate. The upper points of both triangles are attached to a bar which runs across and above the foot. As this bar rests against, and will rub, your boot at the front of the foot, it is covered in leather. This stirrup almost completely covers the foot and thus protects it from being crushed by ranch stock, walls, trees, gates, or any other object that may come into forceful contact with your foot.

Another point to bear in mind is that the stirrups cannot be run up the leathers; whenever you lead a saddled horse, the stirrups will be dangling by his sides and you must be aware that these large, heavy stirrups could get caught on anything – or anybody. When carrying the saddle, the job is made much easier if the stirrups are kept out of your way. The leather thongs used for tying items of clothing or blankets to the saddle can be used to tie the stirrups up, or the stirrups can be crossed over the saddle and interlocked but, after a while, the metal edges of the stirrups start to cut into the cantle.

The crupper (*baticola*) should be made of soft, smooth, well-oiled leather. The rolled part of the crupper that goes around the underside of the tail against the quarters is known as the *morcilla*. The crupper strap runs along the backbone, under the saddle, up through a slot in the saddle, and along the gullet underneath the sheepskin seat. It then comes back on itself and either buckles on the girth or splits into two like a snake's tongue and buckles-up under and in front of the girth either side of the centre. The crupper is essential to the *vaquera* saddle as it helps to stabilize it during the more complicated and faster movements.

There are a number of leather straps that hang from various points on the saddle, which not only hold the sheepskin seat in place, but can also be used to tie down the saddle bags at the back of the saddle and the *manta estribera*, a folded woollen blanket, at the front of the saddle.

There is also a heavy-duty plaited leather strap with a large knot on the end which is attached to the nearside of the saddle, towards the back. This is used occasionally by some, to assist mounting. Mounting blocks are not always readily available in the country!

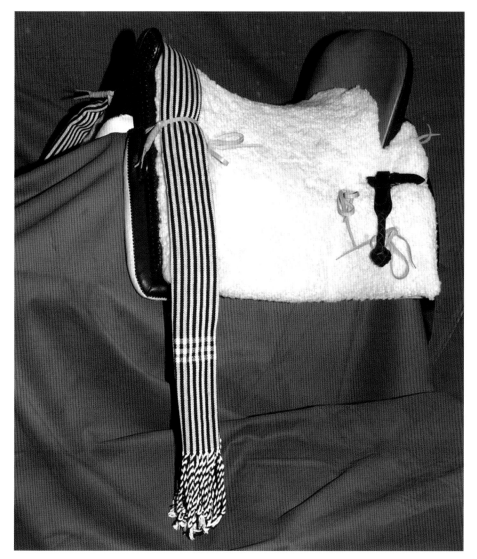

Vaquera saddle, complete with manta estribera.

For work and competition the *vaquera* rider will ride many different horses. The broad Pure-bred Spanish and the narrower Hispano Arabe and Tres Sangres are the most common types of horse used for *vaquera* work. Even so, a *vaquera* rider could get by with just one saddle because the simple design of the *vaquera* saddle means that it can fit almost any well-conformed riding horse. A new saddle sits high and does not bear down on even the highest of Thoroughbred withers, but after many years of wear the way the saddle fits might need to be looked at carefully.

For *vaquera* competition the saddle should be plain black with just a lighter colour, perhaps tan, for the inside of the cantle. Women competitors, where they do compete in this discipline, use the same saddle as the men or, if they prefer, a *vaquera* side-saddle, known as an *Amazona*.

For everyday training, I am inclined, as are many of the Spanish, to use good dressage saddles. This way, particularly in the early stages of training, it is possible to get off a horse's back, especially in the trot, and so produce three good gaits. In competition, only the walk and canter are used, but the trot is important for the overall development of any horse.

Woman rider in a vaquera *side-saddle.*

Getting accustomed to the *vaquera* saddle

Take care when introducing your horse to this saddle. To begin with, it would be wise to lunge the horse with the crupper attached loosely (but not too loose) and with no stirrups on the saddle. Very few riding horses nowadays are used to a crupper, and they can react to it adversely the first few occasions they have one on. You must then judge your horse's progress. As when introducing a horse to any saddle, you must be sure that he has a strong, well-toned back, do not ride him for too long the first time he wears it, and introduce it slowly to avoid him getting a sore back from unfamiliar pressures.

If you have never experienced a *vaquera* saddle before, the first thing you will notice is the softness of the seat. The warmth of the sheepskin is an added benefit in winter, but remember that it has to be kept clean. The second thing you will notice, if you have a new saddle, is that the horse seems to be a long way away from you; you feel very high in the seat. New saddles take years for the casual rider to bed-in but the more you ride, the better it gets. In addition, there are no saddle flaps to close your knees onto, which for some can be a little disconcerting. So plan your own introduction to the saddle carefully, and take some instruction if you need it; this will be of benefit to both you and the horse. This saddle will take a while to feel familiar but, when it does, most people find it an absolute pleasure to ride in.

The *Vaquera* Bridle

The bridle is made of leather with black iron buckles. It has a single rein (*reinda*) attached to a curb bit (*bocado*), which is also made of black iron. The average curb bit has the same dimensions as that of a curb in a double bridle, although the bit shanks can be longer and the ports can vary in height. I hope that riders who are unaccustomed to these bits will acquire a good understanding of how they work and the influence they have on the horse; they require a light hand on the reins and are definitely not for the ham-fisted.

Today it is unusual, in most European countries, to ride with a curb alone. The places you will see this most commonly outside Spain are the ranching communities of the Americas, where, like Spain, the horse is still relied on heavily for work, and a rider needs the right hand free for roping and other activities.

Attached to the bridle's browband (*frontalera*) is the *mosquero* (fly switch), which is secured by two leather thongs pushed through holes in the centre. *Mosqueros* can be made of plain leather or different coloured horse-hair hand-woven into the most intricate and beautiful designs. When the horse is moving at a full *vaquera* walk, the *mosquero* should swing from side to side across the face like a metronome.

Vaquera riders use two styles of bridle: one with a throatlash and one without. On the former, the headpiece with the throatlash (*ahogadero*) buckles to the cheekpieces (*carilleras*) on both sides. The bridle without the throatlash does not require a headpiece and so the cheekpiece strap buckles to the bit on the offside, runs over the head and buckles to the nearside cheekpiece.

There is a possibility that bridles without a throatlash will be pulled off more easily in difficult circumstances, or shaken off by horses whose bridle headpiece sits quite high because they have very thick mane hair. Losing a bridle this way is, however, a very rare occurrence. *Clasica* riders also often use a bridle without a throatlash.

Further down the bridle lies the noseband (*muserola*), which runs through loops formed by the cheekpieces as they pass through holes at the top of the bit shanks and then buckle to themselves. This positioning puts the noseband at the level of a drop noseband, and to ensure that it does not drop too low and hamper the breathing, some riders use a fine piece of leather that runs from the headpiece at the poll, down the centre of the face, and attaches to and supports the noseband. Because the noseband is supported by the cheekpieces, it does not require a headpiece.

The reins, when new, are laced together so that the last 30 cm (1 ft) or so becomes one rein, and you must, when they have been oiled and are soft, wrap the end around itself twice thus making a loop, and push the end through the loop to form a knot.

The *Serreta*

In the right hands the *serreta* is a tool for achieving tremendous control but, like any such tools, it can be abused, which reminds me of the saying: 'A scalpel in the hands of a surgeon can produce great work. In the hands of a maniac it can do great damage.'

The *serreta* is a curved metal bar with a serrated edge that should be shaped to fit snugly over the nasal bone at the level of a drop noseband. You may notice when you fit this for the first time that the arch of the nosepiece is too curved and only touches the horse's nose on the edges of the bone. *Serretas* do not come in standard shapes and sizes, and so to ensure that yours fits your horse's nose, you can place it on an anvil or similar solid item and shape it carefully with a hammer by hitting it near the middle, but not on the rings. With care you can flatten the front, shaping it to the profile of your individual horse. While this requires a modest degree of confidence and competence, it is not very difficult to do, and it is important that the *serrata* is a good fit. If it does not fit snugly, it may slide around the nose as it is used, and this is not desirable.

The plain *serreta* is fitted under the noseband by means of two loops stitched to the outside of the *serreta* through which the noseband passes; it should be padded on the nose side and covered with thick leather. For basic training, a *serreta* can have either one ring to take a lunge rein, or three rings to take side reins and a lunge rein (see Chapter 9).

Rejoneo Tack

The *rejoneador's* saddle is the *vaquera* saddle, but some *rejoneadors* prefer to have an addition at the front of the saddle, sometimes called a gallery (*galeria*); this supports the rider's upper thigh in the fast turns and fast halts.

The bridle, also, would be the same as the *vaquera* bridle, but the *rejoneador* tends to favour the bridle without the throatlash.

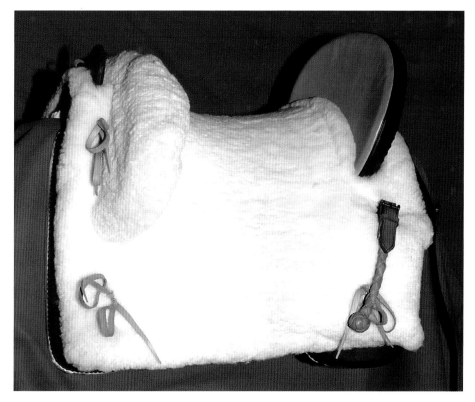

A rejoneador's *saddle, complete with gallery – see text.*

Doma Clasica Tack

The *Doma Clasica* Saddle

The *silla española* (Spanish saddle) is the saddle most commonly used in *doma clasica* and, fundamentally, it is the same saddle as that used by the Royal School in Jerez and the Spanish Riding School of Vienna. There are, however, a number of variations in design and colour available now, although the suede or leather seat under the sheepskin is seldom seen, which is probably just as well because there are some horrendous alternative colours on the market. The Royal School in Jerez uses saddles without the sheepskin, showing a conservative dove-grey suede. To confuse matters, manufacturers might give the typical *clasica* saddle different names, and the specific features of the saddle may have different dimensions.

The *clasica* saddle has, in principle, a seat very similar to that of the continental dressage saddle from the pommel through the seat to the cantle. It is at the cantle, in fact, that the obvious difference between these saddles occurs. The *clasica* cantle is a separate curved panel approximately 10 cm (4 in) high that is attached behind the seat; in this position it is able to support the rider when necessary in the airs above the ground. A panel similar to the gallery on

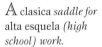

A clasica *saddle for* alta esquela *(high school) work.*

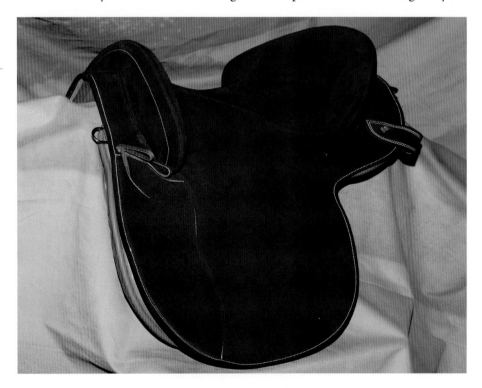

the *rejoneo* saddle is placed at the front and has the same use of supporting the thighs, particularly in the leaps where the rider is thrown up and forwards.

It is usual for the *clasica* saddle to have a breastplate and a crupper. The breastplate, which can be in red and gold, or certain other colours, adds a splash of colour as well as serving its practical function of preventing the saddle from slipping back. The crupper has the same function as that on the *vaquera* saddle but is attached to a metal ring in the centre of the back of the saddle. The *doma clasica* saddle should, like the *vaquera* saddle, have a *manta estribera* tied to it at the front. This will be woollen and, for *clasica*, should be mainly of a single colour with perhaps a stripe or stripes running across it, near to each end. This *manta estribera* matches the saddle cloth. The stirrup leathers are similar in design to those of a Continental dressage saddle, but the stirrups most commonly used are of black iron – less commonly chromed or gold-coloured. They are shaped with flutes, have a swivel for the leather to run through and have flat footplates with shaped sides. The girth is usually two- or three-fold leather, although occasionally white canvas webbing is used, which can look more discreet on a white (grey) horse. These accoutrements complete the picture of elegance and timeless tradition.

The *Doma Clasica* Bridle

The *doma clasica* bridle is always a double bridle. Again, the bits are black iron. Both the bradoon and the curb are of the same proportions as those of the bits used for competition dressage and are, therefore, not more severe, as some people seem to think. I have occasionally had to show people the Spanish bridle next to the familiar double bridle so that they can see for themselves that there is no difference in the bits.

The leatherwork, however, is different from that of the *vaquera* bridle previously described. As there are two bits, there must be two headpieces and two sets of cheekpieces. The curb headpiece buckles on the nearside at the horse's eye level; the second headpiece, carrying the bradoon, runs under the curb headpiece and buckles on the offside. The noseband is also supported by the cheekpieces; the point of the noseband is fed through a keeper inside the offside curb cheekpiece, over the nose and through another keeper on the nearside and does up on the nearside. The noseband is higher in this bridle than the *vaquera* bridle; its height is, in fact, governed by the height of the curb bit as the keepers are fixed. This bridle will also be used without a throatlash, but occasionally some choose to have one for the reasons given earlier when discussing the *vaquera* bridle.

Although the curb cheekpieces hold the noseband firmly in place, the bradoon cheekpieces could not do this because the movement of the bradoon would be seriously limited, thus hindering the correct action. For this reason, you cannot use this kind of bridle with just a snaffle, as some have tried to do by removing the bradoon headpiece and attaching a snaffle to the curb headpiece.

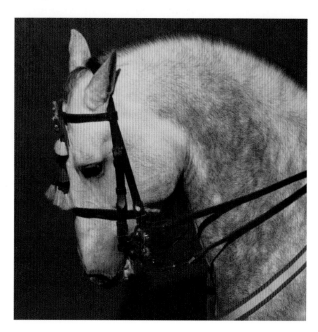

Belinda Joyce's Spanish stallion, Gringo, in a typical clasica *double bridle.*

Costume

The traditional Spanish riding costumes are tailored to set a standard of elegance and poise in both the *vaquera* and the *clasica* classes, and are guaranteed to cut a dash at any fiesta.

Even those of us who are not blessed with the perfect proportions of slender youth can look and feel good, standing proud in these traditional costumes. When they are carefully chosen and *correctly worn* they will enhance almost any shape and size, with only a few exceptions.

Willy Poole wrote an interesting article some years ago in *Horse and Hound* having seen the Spanish show classes at The Royal Windsor Horse Show. He made a critical observation, and said something to the effect that: 'Spanish costumes were designed for lean, mean Latins, not fat Anglo-Saxons, hanging onto their horses by their spurs.' It is true that nothing looks worse than a grossly overweight novice rider crammed into an ill-fitting, creased

Spanish suit, held together by a thin, overtight waistband, with unkempt hair spilling from beneath a hat which is tilted back on the head – and this is why I emphasized 'correctly worn' above; good posture can counteract many a conformation fault. I have seen many a well-rounded Spanish *caballero* who just melted into a shape of effective grace in this costume. However, these men were born to ride and any roundness comes from the advancing years; years which have also borne the fruit of experience and the accomplishment of balance.

The amazing thing about a Spanish costume is, that when it is worn correctly and with an air of inoffensive arrogance, you cannot help but stand taller; and when astride a Spanish horse, you sit deeper with your back straighter, your chest up and your head held high. To complete the picture, your hat is tilted forward and to the right, with the inner edge of the crown touching your eyebrow. This is an artist's dream: a blend of straight lines and curves that form a never-ending opportunity for inspiration; something I see at every show we do when I look at my partner Danielle and admire the beauty and elegance of this form.

Outside Spain and Portugal (see Chapter 8) it is easy to make mistakes when wearing traditional costume. Whilst this is not intentional, a mix of costume styles can be seen as ignorant or even offensive by certain Spanish and Portuguese visitors to our show classes or any other event. Common faults are those as simple as wearing English riding boots and spurs in a costume class or perhaps using Spanish items with your Portuguese outfit.

Many years ago I was pulled aside by Juan Llamas at the Spanish Embassy in London where we were promoting his marvellous book, *This is the Spanish Horse*; this polite and charming man found a way of telling me in a somewhat light-hearted way that I was wearing my costume incorrectly. I had only three, not five, *caireles* (decorative fasteners – see page 90) on my trousers. The fact that the Spanish manufacturers sold these trousers complete with only three did not impress him one bit. Such was my respect for this man and his vast knowledge of all things Spanish, that I never made the mistake again.

Confusion about Iberian equitation can be compounded by thoughtless portrayal in the press. I once opened a well-known horsy magazine to find a picture of my friend Jeff Edwards in full traditional Portuguese riding costume astride his pure-bred Lusitano, Xenofonte, in correct Portuguese tack. The caption stated quite clearly that it was a Spanish horse and rider! We have also had a picture of Danielle in full costume on one of our Spanish stallions, Cartujano, in an article about Lusitanos. These incidents are very frustrating for us and do nothing to promote the right image.

I think these examples illustrate the importance of presenting yourself and your horse impeccably and correctly in order to try to stop this misinformation being perpetuated. However, even in Spain and Portugal you will see an array of variations on a theme which may not be entirely accurate. You could even go into a specialist shop, ask for a complete costume and find it nearly impossible to get the knowledgeable advice that is so important for any equestrian class or event where tradition and etiquette are paramount.

Doma Vaquera Clothing for the *Campo* (Country)

The stockman's riding wear is basically the same as the *doma vaquera* costume for competition (see next section) with one or two variations.

TROUSERS

The trousers are, more often than not, made of a grey material with a darker stripe running through it. A stockman folds the bottoms of his trousers up when riding to show the white lining and the leather *botas de campo* (country boots); they are turned back down when the rider is off the horse. Only trousers without *caireles* (see page 90) can be turned back in this way.

Two different styles of doma vaquera *trousers and footwear: on the right, turned up trousers with* botas de campo; *on the left,* polainas *(half chaps) with* caireles.

BOOTS

The country boots are comfortable from the moment you first buy them. When they are well broken in, they tend to crease at the ankle just enough to allow ease of movement when both riding and walking. This boot is shorter than either the Continental dressage boot or the typical English hunting boot but, as the *vaquera* saddle does not have flaps, the tops of the boots do not pinch the inner calf as they would on a saddle with flaps.

ZAHONES

Zahones are the all-leather, full batwing-shaped chaps (*chaparreros*) that are worn when working with stock in the fields to protect the rider's legs and trousers from cuts, scratches and tears inflicted by anything he may have to ride up against or through. This practical item can be expensive but, for the real stockman, it is an essential investment. The chaps are often decorative, with intricate and finely carved shapes cut out to reveal white leather under-neath. Plaited leather thongs secure the *zahones* by wrapping around the waist like a belt, threading through a slot and being tied to fit the individual rider's dimensions. The top of the *zahones* can then be folded down over the thongs. Leather straps attached to the outer sides of the leg pieces go under the leg just above the knee and fasten to the inner sides of the leg pieces. This inner fastening does not rub the leg because there are no saddle flaps to cause any friction. *Zahones* are not worn in competition as the judges cannot see the aids clearly; they are only for work, fiestas and the bullring.

Doma vaquera *costume showing the addition of a coat rolled inside out and tied over the* manta estribera*.*

COAT

In the country the traditional *manta estribera* (see page 79) might be replaced by a corduroy or woollen hip-length coat that is neatly rolled up, laid across the front of the saddle and tied in place, ready for any adverse weather or a night out under the stars.

Doma Vaquera Costume for Competition

The *traje corto*, the costume of the country, is as meticulous as it is simple; it should not have any fancy adornments or embellishments, the colours are generally sombre and the patterns, if any, are not elaborate. The impression given should simply be one of a country *jinete* dressed up for an occasion.

Below, I have listed the items of the costume in the order in which I would put them on. When the judges and spectators await, you need to know the quickest and least strenuous method of dressing; not everyone can afford a dresser and not all countries have the same casual attitude to performance times as the Spanish.

Undergarments

Suitable undergarments are the first important consideration, for both men and women, if any serious riding is to be done; any unsupported personal equipment will be most uncomfortable, particularly in the fast halts and pirouettes, even when they are planned. Choose undergarments that are soft, comfortable, will not rub and provide the best support possible.

Socks or stockings should be cream or beige and stretch to above the knee, so that a hint of their colour shows through the openings in the *polainas* (half chaps).

Shirt

The shirt is always white, simple and plain, with no patterns or lace frills. It is worn without a tie, neatly done up at the collar; the *vaquera* rider's shirt should never be undone when riding. The shirt cuffs should show beneath the jacket cuffs and often 'Sunday best' cufflinks are worn.

Trousers

The trousers are high-waisted and come to the base of the ribcage; they are usually black, or grey with a fine stripe (not unlike the trousers worn with an English morning suit). They are close-fitting around the seat and thighs and are shorter than would normally be expected from suit trousers. The shorter length ensures that, when the wearer is walking, the trouser legs do not reach the heel and are thus kept out of the dust.

The only adornment that is acceptable is in the form of *caireles*. These are exquisite silver acorns, stirrups or horse heads, five in total, that hang on slender chains at the base of the trouser legs. Each *cairele* fits into a button hole and it is important to remember that the top two close the split in the trouser leg, the bottom three being left undone to allow the trouser to open slightly, displaying the *polainas* (see below).

The trouser fly can be either button or zip fastening and should have a piece of cloth that is stitched firmly to the left and comes across the stomach to button on the right as a support for the zip or fly buttons. As you can imagine, this area comes under considerable stress during *vaquera* riding. The trousers are held up by braces, which, when made of carved leather, can mirror the carved work on the *polainas*.

Once you have your shirt and trousers on, a useful tip is to leave your braces down and the front of the trousers undone because the time spent folded in half over your knees while putting on your boots and *polainas* will be far less painful, especially after a hearty lunch and a glass or two of Rioja. Trust me, I speak from experience.

*D*oma vaquera *costume, showing* caireles *and* polainas *(see text).*

SHOES AND BOOTS

In competition, the *vaquera* rider wears either the *vaquera* shoes, which lace up, or short boots (similar to jodhpur boots), which have elasticated sides. It is important to put the shoes or boots on before the *polainas*, which can then be put on over the footwear. Doing it the other way round is more complicated.

POLAINAS

The *polainas* can be carved, like the *zahones*, and have other decorative leatherwork, which has a practical use; it both does up the half-chaps and adjusts them. Neatly shaped flaps loop through each other from the bottom of the *polaina* to three-quarters of the way up, then a final knotted leather strap slips through a shaped eyelet to hold the top in place above the calf. This strap also adjusts the tightness at the top. The whole item is made completely of leather; no buckles or buttons, zips or Velcro, just truly traditional leather craftsmanship.

SPURS

The next items to go on are the black iron spurs (*espuelas*) which have either white or brown leather straps. The strap is run through three slots in the spur: one at the back and one on either side. If the spur arms are straight, it does not matter which spur goes on which foot, but occasionally they curve in and then it is obvious which spur belongs where. There are two important things to remember about the fitting of the spurs: one is that the spur-strap buckle is not to be seen and so must do up on the inside of your foot; and the other is that the spur should always be worn at the lowest point, in line with the heel of the boot. In this position the spur gives the subtle rider the chance to vary its use. By adjusting the angle and action of the foot and lower leg, you can stroke the spur forwards or backwards, or close the spur in, etc., thus achieving myriad effects from relaxation to immediate impulsion.

(Nuno Oliveira commented on the way many modern competition dressage riders wear their spurs too high, some wearing them as high as the ankle. This, he said, leaves very little opportunity to vary the use of the spur. Watching many riders, it certainly appears that the spur is either on or off the horse, with no subtle use in between.)

Espuelas usually have rowels, which are manufactured with sharp points, and I always file the points smooth. My advice is that the rowels should always be filed unless you are totally confident that you can keep your legs very still in all movements, and that when you do apply the spurs, if they are required, you apply them with the minimum amount of force for any given aid or situation.

WAISTBAND

The colourful silk waistband can be purchased ready made for the job, like a cummerbund, or you could use something that is most fashionable: a lady's headscarf, which is folded diagonally, rolled up, then wrapped around your waist and knotted. The ends should be discreetly tucked in, not left hanging down your thigh in the style of a Mexican bandit.

JACKET AND WAISTCOAT

The short jacket (*chaquetilla*) has a round, low collar. To match the number of *caireles* on the trousers, there are five buttons on the front of the jacket – but only the top one should be done up – and five buttons on each cuff. The jacket should fit snugly and have clean lines, particularly the shoulders, which must have crisp angles; no soft, puffy, home-made, wrinkly extremities.

A number of colours are acceptable for the jacket, popular colours being various shades of grey, light blue, dark blue, burgundy, khaki and brown. Black will only be seen occasionally, usually for a complete suit, and can look very smart for exhibitions, but would never be seen in competition. When patterned materials are chosen, the pattern must be subtle – for example, where checks and stripes are used they are only noticeable close up. Suits of one colour are worn and the colour is sometimes representative of an area of Spain, although nowadays it is more likely to be personal choice that governs the selection of a colour.

The waistcoat is short but it goes over the waistband, and it must match the jacket.

HAT

Finally we come to the wide-brimmed hat (*sombrero*), which, over the years, has changed quite dramatically and in crown height and style. Today, it is a familiar and practical shape designed to keep the strong Spanish sun off the face and out of the eyes. Hats, again, come in a number of acceptable colours, the most popular being grey, ranging from a dark charcoal grey with a white band around the crown and the brim edge, to a uniform light grey.

The *sombrero*, unlike the Stetson the cowboys of the Americas wear, is the last thing you should put on and the first thing you take off. But the cowboys would definitely agree with the *vaquera* riders that the one time a hat should be removed is when a lady is present. For the Spanish stockmen, removing the hat when a *señora* or *señorita* approaches makes it easier to take advantage of the charming social

The complete traje corto, *the costume of the country, seen from behind.*

activity of the kiss on both cheeks – one of the few pleasures left for the older *caballero*! The hair must be smartly trimmed.

To ensure that your hat stays on your head, shorten the chin strap until it is tight on your chin by placing the strap at the end of your chin with your jaw relaxed. Mark the place on the strap and sew across it at what is the correct length for you. When you pick up speed, you set you jaw against the strap and your hat stays on your head, and does not fall behind it. This is unsightly and embarrassing; almost as embarrassing as when you lose your hat completely and then ride straight over it the next time around the arena.

WOMEN'S *DOMA VAQUERA* COSTUME FOR COMPETITION

Women's outfits are basically the same as those of the men and should mostly match the sober colours of the men's costumes; if they ride side-saddle on an *Amazona* saddle the trousers are replaced with a long side-saddle skirt (in England, this is called a habit) in black or grey. Flamboyant earrings are out of place. The hair must be neat: either pulled back and tied with a dark ribbon or worn in a bun. Flowers, brightly coloured ribbons or other hair decorations are not permitted. Women have a choice of hat styles; they either wear the typical *sombrero español de ala ancha*, or the *calañes* or *catite*, which are the smaller, rounder styles of hat.

The *vaquera* costume must be clean, pressed and correct in every way; your horse, the judge, the spectators and, above all, the *vaquera* culture will then be paid the homage they deserve.

Rejoneo Costume

The *rejoneador* has a choice: he can either wear the *vaquera* costume with the *zahones* or the *clasica* costume (see below) with *zahones*, but his overall outfit will be a little more extravagant than these other styles .

The jacket is always of the same practical cut for riding but it can have the most exquisite embellished stitching along the back, elbows and cuffs, in an intricate design. The jacket collars and lapels can vary; they are either the same as those on a man's double-breasted lounge suit, or they are cut straight down the side and rounded in front of the chest. The waistcoat must match the colour of the jacket.

The shirt is much like those used with evening dress and tuxedos, being often frilled with lace and having silver or mother-of-pearl buttons.
The hat is the same as the *vaquera* hat.

Doma Clasica Costume

The more fashionable costume for the traditional *clasica* competitions is the same as that described for the *rejoneador*.

A selection of stylish jackets can be worn by the *clasica* rider, under which he wears a white, frilled shirt and waistcoat; again, the waistcoat must match the jacket.

Black trousers with *caireles* are traditional for *clasica* events, as are spurs with plain brown straps; the white spur straps worn in *vaquera* events are out of place in *clasica* events.

The costume style often favoured by the Royal Andalusian School (although it does have a varied wardrobe) is the Goyesque; black breeches with *polainas* and very dark boots will be worn, with a little stocking showing above the *polainas*. *Zahones* are not worn. The jackets match the waistcoats, both of which being very decorative, embroidered in exquisite gold thread.

A Domecq stallion in pesade in the Andalusian countryside: the rider is wearing the Goya costume of the Andalusian School of Equestrian Art.

Danielle Lawniczak riding Lorraine Ould's Spanish stallion, Zurito, in a typical doma clasica *outfit.*

The shirt is white and a scarf is worn around the neck. The hat, which is of a traditional shape, is carefully chosen to match the outfit.

In Spain you will occasionally see a mixture of the *vaquera* and *clasica* styles but for me there is nothing more impressive than a traditional *clasica* turnout.

Presentation of the Horse

Trimming

For *doma vaquera* in particular, a horse, like a rider, demonstrating his abilities before judges and spectators must be presented well. The picture must be one of neat, workmanlike elegance; the horse must be clean and there must not be a hair out of place. With some horses, this may mean removal of hair. The ears are trimmed very close to the skin both inside and on the edges; all hair under the chin, long hair on the legs and feather on the fetlocks must be removed. This is easy to do and in my opinion gives almost any riding horse a touch of extra quality.

When a horse has either a docked tail or a cut tail (see below), it is normal to trim the whole forelock to the point behind the ears where the bridle sits, and then the pulled mane can be plaited for special occasions or left conveniently short during training.

Plaiting the Mane

If a Pure-bred Spanish stallion is being presented (which is not as common as the more-favoured part-breds), it is a shame to pull his mane and so with a thick, long mane we can plait in large plaits, starting at the forelock and moving down the neck, folding the plaits up to about 8 cm (3 in), or alternatively in the running plait described in the section on Plaiting the Mane of the

Vaquera plaits.

Clasica Horse. With finer manes it is sometimes possible to plait into small buttons like the plaits used in England for hunting and show classes.

One of the most important things to remember before you start plaiting, or taking up the tail in *sevillana* style, is not to spray with conditioner first. The hair will spring out of place the minute your back is turned. On the contrary, it can help to wet the tail or the mane; it will be easier to handle and the plaits will stay in longer and be tighter.

PLAITING THE MANE OF THE *REJONEO* HORSE

This highly decorative mane dressing is reserved for fiestas and the bullring; it has no place in *doma vaquera* competition. The mane is threaded with coloured ribbons of a stiff material (which have also been well-starched and ironed) approximately 10 cm (4 in) in width, and long enough to run from the withers to the poll and back to the withers with some ribbon to spare. Two colours are very fashionable: red and gold (these being the colours in the Spanish flag); but there are a number of other colour combinations used as well.

The mane must first be split in half down the full length of the neck in the centre, to fall evenly on either side of the neck. Wet the mane and do a running plait down each side. Once the plaits are finished and fastened with elastic bands, you can start to thread the ribbons through the plaits. Fold the starched and ironed ribbons in half from end to end, having marked the centre of each with a crease so that you have an equal length of ribbon for both sides. Starting at the head, thread the first colour in loops through the plait, take the first colour through the plait on the other side and then repeat with the second ribbon. The only way to achieve a really neat finish with this is to practise the exercise frequently. See photos opposite.

PLAITING THE MANE OF THE *CLASICA* HORSE

The *clasica* horse will have his mane presented in one of two ways. If he is being presented in the style of the Royal Andalusian School the horse might have a single running plait down one side. For a dressage competition in English tack, the horse will have the single running plait with the forelock plaited in a French plait (i.e. plaited like a tail plait with strands of hair being taken in from the outside), or the more usual ball plait. If the mane is very thick it is permissible to do the double plait as described above. For display purposes the *clasica* horse's plaits can be adorned with red and gold or white and green bobbles, usually in three groups of three bobbles. See photos on pages 100–1.

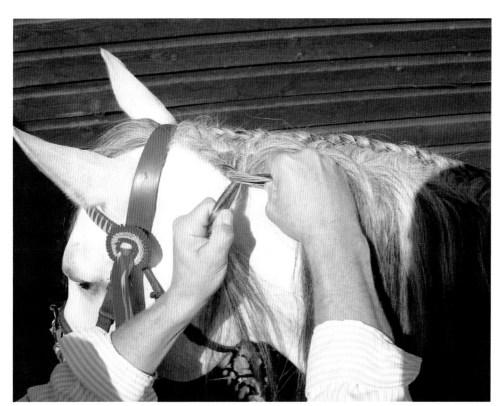

The initial process of double plaiting rejoneo style.

HERE AND OPPOSITE
ABOVE

*Creating running
plaits.*

The finished running plait.

Dressing the Tail

There are basically three styles of tail dressing; the first two being specifically for *doma vaquera*.

The docked tail which, incidentally, is a practice the English introduced to Spain when fighting Napoleon, is now illegal in Britain and is found less frequently in Spain. A better practice, and the second style, is to cut the tail straight across just beneath the end of the dock.

If you have a horse with a full tail and want to keep it that way, the third style is essential for *doma vaquera*. It is just one of a number of interesting methods of dressing the tail, and can also be used for carriage horses and for horses who do the airs above the ground.

It is not easy to do and many people take a while to master this Spanish method of dressing the tail without using needles, thread, elastic bands, tape, or Blu-tack. The easiest way to learn this method is by practical demonstration but the following text and photographs outline the basic technique.

You start by separating a slender group of hairs that grow from the base of the dock from the bulk of the tail. Leaving the separated group hanging, twist the bulk of the tail clockwise until the hair at the end of the dock begins to form a single loop or bun. Then take the hair anticlockwise, spiralling upwards around the tail once, or twice if the length allows. Holding this firmly with the left hand, take the separated hair still hanging under the bottom bun shape over and round, then on the second turn go diagonally, spiralling upwards clockwise until you have a thick band of hair and a thin one ready to cross over.

This is when it gets complicated and you feel the need for a third hand. Taking the last 8 cm (3 in) of the thick band you twist a few more times in the same original direction and fold in half. Holding this folded hair as firmly as you can, and keeping everything as tight as possible, take the last 8–10 cm (3–4 in) of the thin hairs and spiral them tightly around, continuing in the clockwise direction. It is important that you start at the fold and spiral down towards the tail itself; this will tighten the knot. The last thing to do is to take the thin strands running diagonally across, lift them a little and push the knot under them. You can then slide the whole thing down the tail to tighten it.

It is important to remember that when you teach rein-back, pirouettes and piaffe, the horse's haunches should lower and a long tail can be trodden on, causing large clumps of hair to be pulled out. Therefore, use this method of

OPPOSITE AND OVERLEAF *The process of dressing the tail.*

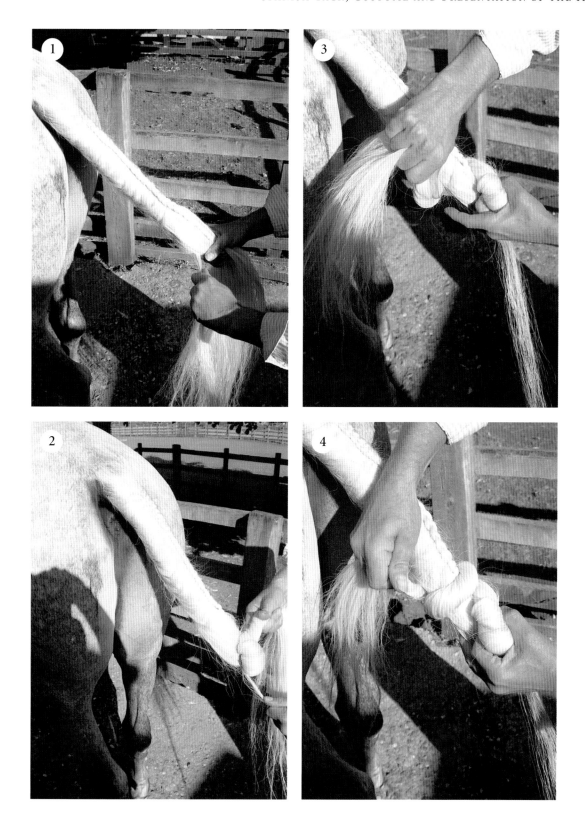

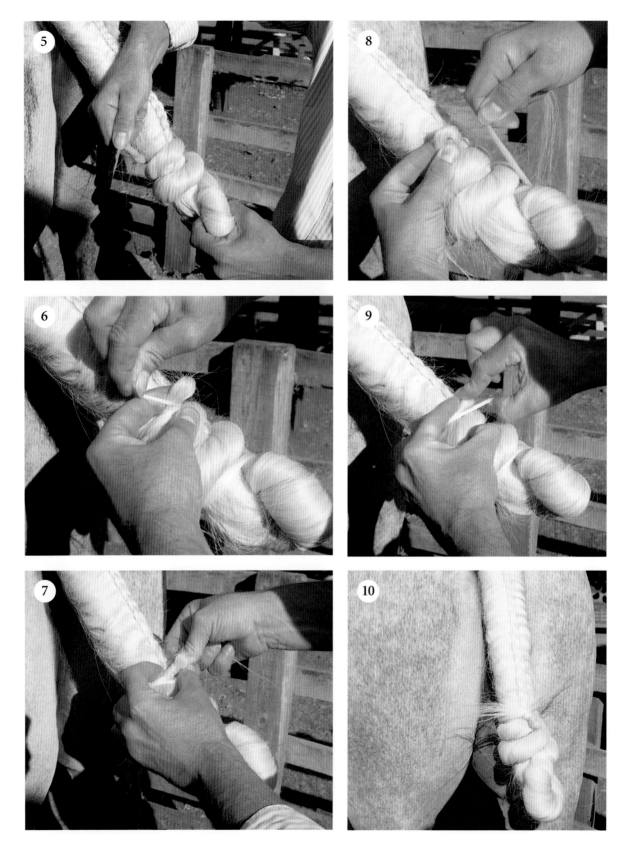

tying the tail to prevent this hair loss or, perhaps to avoid a flick in the face from the tail when working the horse in-hand or helping a friend from the ground.

Always remove plaits and banged tails at the earliest opportunity as, if left in (overnight, for example), they will irritate the horse and he may rub out the hairs, leaving you with an unsightly mess. The hairs may take a long time to grow back and you will not be able to plait or dress the horse properly in the near future. Treat all manes and tails with care, and do not use dandy brushes on them. Also, whenever possible, just run you fingers through the hair rather than using combs; this way your horses will keep their crowning glories.

Chapter Eight

The Pride of Portugal

WHILST THIS BOOK IS primarily about the Spanish horse, the Portuguese horse has, I believe, a valid place in it. The Lusitanos' history is so closely intertwined with that of the Andalusian: essentially they are the same horse; they have the same evolution and heritage, and the differences they do have are the result of selective breeding in modern times. The breed is every bit The Pride of Portugal as the Andalusian is The Legend of Spain.

I have appreciated, worked with, promoted and presented the Lusitano since I met Jeffery Edwards about fifteen years ago at The British Andalusian Horse Society Annual Breed Show. We were both competing in a riding class in full costume; Jeffery was riding Xenofonte, his Lusitano, and I was on Chico, my Hispano Arabe.

Watching this pair work was a revelation. What struck me was not so much the actual riding ability, which undoubtedly stood above everyone else's, but more the image of calmness and serenity this partnership brought to the arena.

Xenofonte was a tall Veiga-bred Lusitano who had an amazing ability to draw you immediately into his eyes; they stood out from his noble head as if carved by a Greek mason over two and a half thousand years ago – which may be what influenced the choice of his name. When Xenofonte walked you were totally captivated, almost hypnotized, by the rhythm and grace as he moved with such elegance, elevation and precision, as if he were climbing a glass staircase.

There is nothing flashy, flamboyant or arrogant about Jeff's riding; he is

the humblest of horseman. There is, however, a quiet, knowledgeable softness about him that guides this sensitive and energetic horse through every performance, making the simplest of movements every bit as beautiful as the most complicated. Herein lies one of the profound secrets of the equestrian art.

On the day I first saw this partnership I made a point of seeking Jeff out and invited him to join my display team, El Caballo de España. He immediately accepted and a great and loyal friendship started that day, as did our contribution to promoting the Lusitano in England. For both of us it was just a turn of fate that dictated whether it was a Lusitano or Andalusian with whom we first became associated. I have since spent many enjoyable hours in Jeff's and the Lusitano's company and learnt a great deal from both.

Since the formation of The Lusitano Breed Society of Great Britain and The British Andalusian Horse Society, as they were then known, the two organizations have operated side by side, with many of the same views and aims and, in some cases, the same members, who obviously appreciate the qualities of both breeds.

Jeff Edwards' Xenofonte, a Lusitano from the Veiga bloodline, was the epitome of grace and beauty.

On the whole, each group has had a healthy competitive attitude to the promotion of their horses, only occasionally marred, as all these affairs are, by the personal agendas of some and the politics of others. I am pleased to say that here in England the Associations have resisted the temptation to merge.

When you become familiar with these two breeds, you soon realize how much about them is similar – location and history dictate this – yet so much is so different.

In this chapter I have encompassed many aspects of the Lusitano that I have covered for the Spanish horse in the rest of the book. It is my intention to give newcomers an introduction and an insight to the Lusitano breed, encouraging them to look at the horse a little more closely.

BELOW AND OPPOSITE

Three beautiful Lusitano mares owned by Enrique Guerro.

A *group of Enrique Guerro's Lusitano mares.*

Two of a Kind?

There is a lot said about how different Spain and Portugal are and in many ways that is true. One thing sometimes said is that the Spanish breed the better horses and the Portuguese are the better riders; that would be difficult to debate in particular circles. However, there are certainly many other differences in the cultures, traditions and presentation of these horses, even though the horses themselves have so many similarities; in certain cases, only the true aficionados can tell which is which. Even then they may have to check the brands and which side they are on! The Lusitano is branded on the opposite side from the Spanish horse: the male pure-breds should be branded on the offside flank and the females on the nearside. But this is by no means foolproof; occasionally someone gets it wrong, which can be confusing.

Lusitanos can also have a number of other brands on the neck, shoulders, and on the hindquarters just to the side of the tail. These various marks and numbers can indicate, for example, stock from a particular mare and even what year the horse was born. Whilst this can help those who understand the system, everyone else is advised to study the papers.

Grading

Internationally, the Lusitano is controlled by the *Associação Portuguesa de Criadores do Cavalo Puro Sangue Lusitano (APSL)*. This Portuguese government department oversees the protection and development of the Lusitano horse, and is responsible for managing the stud book and defining the breed standards.

The Portuguese stud book, the *Registo Genealógico do Cavalo Puro Sangue Lusitano* was established when it broke away from the *Spanish State Stud Book*. In fact, when you go through the genealogical lines, you will see the same famous stallions cropping up time and time again in both stud books.

The Portuguese include a ridden section for stallions and an in-hand inspection for mares in their grading system. This process is carried out in Portugal and wherever else in the world the Lusitano is found; this is essential to the continued growth of the breed, and maintenance of quality and credibility.

To get all the up-to-date criteria, the where, when and how of registering youngstock and imported stock, or specific information on grading, it is wise to approach the relevant breed society or association that should have a registrar who is knowledgeable and able to advise on, or in fact handle all aspects of, the process.

In most cases the grading happens once a year, usually at central locations, and this can be an opportunity to meet many other breeders. However, the actual grading process may (as I believe it should) be private. When I was President of The British Association for the Purebred Spanish Horse I always insisted that the grading area be cleared, much to the dismay of the occasional unsympathetic onlooker. It was usually those who bought already-graded horses who could not understand why anyone should not wish to be the centre of attraction at that moment of extreme embarrassment and distress when their cherished horse did not pass his grading.

What's in a Portuguese Name?

The Portuguese Pure-bred

The name 'Lusitano' derives from Portugal's old name, Lusitania, and so the Lusitano will also be called the Portuguese horse.

Like the Spanish, the Portuguese cross breed their pure-bred Lusitanos; the most popular crosses being very similar to those of the Spanish: the

Lusitano/Arab and Luistano/Thoroughbred crosses are favourites for ranch work and are also favoured in the bullring for their endurance and their speed for the first part of the mounted bullfight.

The Portuguese also put their pure-breds to many other breeds, in particular heavier types. Some years ago, an immensely strong, agile and exceptionally courageous Lusitano/Percheron cross was a particular favourite in the bullring.

Overall, the qualities the Lusitano brings to a breeding programme equal those of the Andalusian.

THE VEIGA BLOODLINE

The name 'Veiga' is revered in the Lusitano world. Bred for the traits required for the bullring, horses of this famous bloodline have a reputation for fire, energy, spirit and boundless courage. Aesthetically a Veiga may not be as inspiring as some of his brethren from other lines and he is small (15–15.2 hh), but when he faces a bull, this little horse stands very tall indeed. His elegant gaits allow him to carry a rider with grace and he has a phenomenal ability to bring his hocks well beneath his belly. Few other bloodlines can inspire quite so much awe and respect as the Veiga horses.

Opus, the famous bullfighting mount of the equally renowned *rejoneador* Alvaro Domecq, comes from the Veiga line.

THE D'ANDRADE BLOODLINE

Fernando Sommer d'Andrade, the son of Ruy d'Andrade, is considered to be the most influential of Lusitano breeders and is respected as one of the most knowledgeable on the Iberian horse.

The Andrade horse is amongst the most prestigious of Lusitano horses, and owning one should be considered an honour. This stud, like certain old-established studs in Spain, consistently breeds horses of great quality who are the culmination of extensive experience and knowledge passed down through many generations of the family – something which is impossible to emulate solely by the purchase of a few champions.

THE ALTER REAL

The Alter Real is a specific bloodline of the Lusitano, most notably associated with The Portuguese School of Equestrian Art. This horse is always bay in colour and of a particular type: a muscular, powerful back and haunches are carried by strong hocks, facilitating a breathtaking elevation in collection.

The first part of the name is derived from the town of Alter do Chão, in the province of Alentejo, which is home to this breed's national stud; and 'Real', meaning royal, comes from the connection to the House of Braganza, the royal family who founded this stud in 1748. They imported approximately fifty Andalusian mares from Spain for the purpose of breeding carriage and high-school horses for the royal manège in Lisbon.

In the nineteenth century, the Peninsular Wars were the cause of great depletion in the Alter Real stock; many were lost to Napoleon's rampaging army. Post war, breeding declined and attempts to restore the stud with an introduction of blood from northern European horses were in vain. After this the fortunes of the breed fluctuated until the Portuguese republic superseded the monarchy at the beginning of the twentieth century; the new government wanted to close the stud and the breed was all but wiped out. At the eleventh hour one Dr Ruy d'Andrade arrived at the Alter stud to rescue two stallions and just a few mares. Some years later, Dr d'Andrade was able to hand over a small thriving stud of Alter Reals to the Ministry of Agriculture. If it had not been for the foresight of this man, the breed would have been lost for ever.

Some of the famous Portuguese studs and breeders are: Alter Real, Coudelarai Nacional, Fernando Sommer D'Andrade, Infante Da Camara, Manuel Veiga.

The Portuguese Working Horse and Working Equitation

The Portuguese pure-breds and part-breds are still used out in the country but, where the Spanish have developed the skills used in the *campo* in the *doma vaquera* competitions, the Portuguese riders also have Working Equitation competitions.

A serious sport throughout Europe, with Spain, France and Italy already producing some very capable competitors, it is now creating interest in Britain and I am sure that in time it will spread.

The competition is in three parts: dressage, obstacles and stock work (in Britain stock work is not included in the competition). Although the dressage is not generally of the *standard* associated with the higher levels ridden under FEI rules, competitors are required to perform certain *movements* associated with Advanced level. These include lateral work, counter-canter, multiple changes of leg at canter and pirouettes; all of which are additionally put to the test in the obstacle course.

Competitors are expected to carry out various tasks which include: opening and shutting gates without letting go, for which there is a particular technique; bending round poles with changes of leg and demi-pirouettes at canter; full-passing along a pole between the horse's front and back legs; reversing through a right angle; taking a small jump; walking over a wooden bridge; riding around three barrels with a flying change at each change of direction; circling small farm stock in a pen; and picking up a loop on the end of a small javelin, which is similar to the Spanish *garrocha* but smaller. This last test demonstrates the agility and accuracy of the rider.

The stock work comprises rounding up and working cattle.

You can see from this that there are a number of elements in this competition you may see in other activities – the Western trail class and barrel racing, for example – and, perhaps, elements of Handy Hunter classes, tent pegging and Le Trec (a type of orienteering with horses). But, make no mistake, at its best Working Equitation is a fantastic demonstration of versatility and control by both horse and rider.

The Portuguese take immense pride in using Lusitano stock in this interesting and exciting sport. They are also proud of the fact that they usually win, although this may change if other countries take the bull by the horns and produce more competitors!

The Portuguese Bullring

The Lusitano is so interlinked with bullfighting that many breeders think only of the bullring as a test of their horses. Undoubtedly this arena is the ultimate test in courage, strength, agility, power and movement, but it is not, as I have said before, the best criterion for breeding horses for the average Sunday afternoon rider.

Both Spain and Portugal have rules and a code under which bullfighting is conducted, but there are certain differences between them.

In Portugal, bullfighting is always performed mounted and the *cavaleiro*, like the Spanish *rejoneador*, faces the bull on a horse, the favourite breed being, of course, the Lusitano.

The *cavaleiro* faces the same challenges as the *rejoneador* and, in the main, the bull's role in the arena is the same as his Spanish counterpart's. In the extreme movements between horse, horseman and bull there are moments of fantastic artistry and there is an impression of togetherness between horse and rider, each totally focused on the other, totally reliant on each other's existence. The *cavaleiro* and his horse parade, prance and strut before the bull, taunting him and enticing the charge, and it is not until the charge is made that the *cavaleiro* can in fact strike his blow. He may approach in a number of different ways: it may be across the front of the bull or directly from the front, but always at speed and always close enough to feel the bull's breath.

In Spain, the bull is destroyed in the arena, but in Portugal the end differs. Once the bull has been weakened by the *banderillas*, a group of *forcados* enter the arena. These young men may come from any walk of life, but are often the sons of local architects, lawyers or farmers. Dressed in traditional costume, they stand before a weakened but still dangerous and unpredictable beast, and their aim is to subdue him with their bare hands until the president of the bullfight gives his approval of their success.

The *forcados* line up one behind the other, the intention being that the first in line is supported by those behind him. He will then entice the bull to charge and when the bull does so, number one then throws himself on the bull between the horns; the others, hopefully, slow the path of the bull. The last of these brave, or perhaps somewhat coerced men, will grab the tail. Together they bring the bull to a standstill.

Whilst there are eight of these brave young *forcados*, it doesn't always work out in their favour. I did hear a wonderful account of how one particular bull got the best of his particular group of *forcados* (which seems to occur quite often) then jumped out of the arena and proceeded to harass the spectators, no doubt to the delight and amusement of all those watching from a safe distance. How wonderful to see the roles reversed.

The bull is let out of the arena at the end and killed. As in Spain, every so often a bull impresses the crowds so much with his courage that he is allowed freedom. He is patched up and retired to spend the rest of his life grazing and producing more brave bulls.

Portuguese Tack and Costume

The Portuguese traditional tack and costume differ from those of Spain, but the uninitiated might be confused because both countries have followed a similar historical path in both practical and fashion wear. For example, the bright sun of the Iberian summers requires a wide-brimmed hat to protect the eyes when working in the fields all day. I will describe briefly the typical traditional tack and costume used and worn in Portugal, but for those who require a more thorough knowledge, I recommend *O Traje Portugues de*

Equitacão (Portuguese Riding Costume) by Lina Gorjão Clara and João Gorgão Clara. These authors describe and illustrate the deterioration of clothing worn at the *Feira da Golega*, an example of how these wonderful traditions can be lost if the culture is not observed and respected.

Traditional Tack

The saddle

The saddle, whilst having the same fundamental components as the Spanish *clasica* saddle, has a different shape and finish. The seat is principally the same as that of the *clasica* saddle, but usually with a larger pommel, like the gallery on the *rejoneador*'s saddle. The cantle is, again, usually larger, running further round the back of the rider and supporting the thigh more than the standard Spanish *clasica* saddle. The Portuguese saddle is thus useful for work in the field, the bullring or in fact any arena. Another feature that sets it apart is the squared-off bottom to the saddle flap, which is shorter than both the Spanish and the European dressage saddles. In order that the legs do not rub against the girth buckles and girth there is another small, square leather panel which is suspended from the saddle flap by leather straps.

The saddle has a suede seat, and is finished with metal studs at the front of the pommel and the back of the cantle. These silver-coloured, or occasionally gold-coloured, studs are highly decorative. Overall the saddle resembles the great saddle of old, and has hardly changed shape or design for many years, unlike the modern European dressage saddles that are always having details, shapes and materials changed in an effort to improve them and capture a bigger share of the market place.

The visually timeless nature of the Portuguese saddle makes it very popular for film work, since it can fit into so many eras. It is also a tad more secure for the actors, many of whom only get the very basic of crash courses in staying on, before being let loose on the set.

Unfortunately, the Portuguese now make their saddles in the most bizarre reds, purples and other circus-inspired hues to suit the taste of a particular group of people. I believe that the usually accepted colours are still black, brown, fawn and grey, which should complement any colour of horse or costume.

The stirrups can again be highly decorative, a highly polished silver or gold colour, and be one of several patterns and designs, all of which look elegant and like period pieces. The most distinctive are the square stirrups that are so popular and complement all costumes. Those often seen in the bullring are the wooden, box-shaped, embellished stirrups built to protect the rider's foot in the same way as the *vaquera* stirrups do.

Behind the rider, attached to the saddle, is the *charrel*, which is made of an animal skin such as fox. It is attached by leather straps to the back of the saddle and protects the rider's long coat from the grease and dust on the horse's back.

THE BRIDLE

The Portuguese bridles are generally of two types. The plainer bridle, by Portuguese standards, has large silver-coloured or gold-coloured square buckles and usually has stainless steel bits of the same design as those used in any dressage competition where a double bridle is required. You may occasionally see a bit of the same type as a Spanish curb but this will be plated in silver or gold and is never seen in black. These bridles are used as double bridles or with the curb bit only. The noseband runs through the cheekpieces where they buckle to the curb bit. The leatherwork on these bridles is neither carved nor decorated.

In contrast to this, other double bridles are highly decorative, having the most ornate buckles and adornments, and moulded or cast silver-coloured or gold-coloured curb bits.

The Pure-bred Lusitano stallion, Forcado, owned and ridden by El Caballo de España team member Jeff Edwards, in a typical Portuguese bridle.

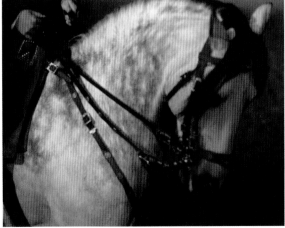

The Pure-bred Lusitano stallion, Negativo, owned and ridden by El Caballo de España team member Jan Hakeney, in a highly decorative Portuguese bridle.

Traditional Costume

JACKET

In my opinion, one of the most distinguished items of clothing is the black jacket neatly cut with double-pointed lapels similar to those seen on a well-cut double-breasted suit. The jacket itself is short, barely covering the ribcage, and is worn over a waistcoat of the same colour and cloth. It can have either plain buttons, or silk or synthetic ornamental buttons, on the front. These can vary tremendously in design and will be influenced by fashion. The sombre colours of these jackets: blacks, greys, browns and so on, are often trimmed with velvet collars and can be edged around the lapels and pockets in another material of a darker colour, or even black.

Some of the more adventurous may have jackets of dog-tooth checks or some similar checked pattern. To ward of the cold the Portuguese also have a selection of overcoats or jackets made of heavier wool, often with a fur collar. One of the most popular and elegant of the heavier coats is a long coat with a shoulder cape which also has a fur collar. They were originally created to protect a rider from the worst of the weather, right down to his boots.

SHIRT

The shirt (*camisa*) is always white and can be as decorative as a gentleman's evening shirt. The Portuguese like to wear these shirts with personalized double collar-links, the designs of which vary tremendously, from simple plain gold studs to initialled enamelled ones.

TROUSERS AND BREECHES

Today, one generally sees the rider in trousers, which is a relatively recent item of riding apparel; previously, breeches were always worn. These were knee length and were covered by silk stockings, normally white or off-white, which were worn over and above the knee. The breeches and stockings are still seen with the jackets described above but are more commonly seen with the more flamboyant eighteenth-century costume used in the bullring and for displays.

The trousers are very similar to the Spanish *vaquera* trousers. These are usually grey with a fine stripe, although a different grey from those worn by the *vaquera* riders, but the trousers can be coloured and often match the waistcoat, which may or may not be the same as the jacket. For example, a grey jacket will be worn with black trousers and waistcoat, or a suit of a matching material and colour may be preferred.

The trouser legs should be long enough to look elegant when dismounted but should ride up the leg enough to expose the boot. They are normally cut straight and cuffless and do not have any adornments. Cut high on the waist, almost to the sternum, they are held up with braces.

BOOTS AND SPURS

There are numerous styles of boots, from the most simple of *campo* boots, coming barely to the top of the calf and cut straight across the top, to the most elegant patent-leather boots which are fastened by means of a system of pins and loops. There are also many designs with various types of side fastenings, and one particular type of boot is worn normally with the eighteenth-century costume.

A characteristic of the Portuguese *campo* boot is that the sole is usually wider than the foot and the shelf-like heel stands out from the foot. This allows a specially designed spur, shaped and slightly sprung, to clip neatly into the welt of the heel. (Spanish boots have the leather sole and heel trimmed flush all the way round and so these spurs would be quite impractical as they would slip and fall off.)

These spurs are very useful because, as stated, they slip on and off easily as you need to use them, which is of real benefit if you are to train several horses a day and need to continually change the type of spur used – from a straight, single-point spur to a rowelled spur, for example – for the particular requirements of each horse. Outside Portugal, however, it is difficult to find

Peter Maddison-Greenwell (LEFT) *riding* Farolero *in* doma vaquera *costume while* Jeff Edwards (RIGHT) *rides his Lusitano,* Xenofonte, *in traditional Portuguese costume.*

either long or short boots that can facilitate these slip-on spurs. Other spurs strap on and come in a number of styles, including sharp rowelled ones.

Polainas

Polainas similar to our leather gaiters are worn with the country outfits and would protect against thorns and bushes whilst out working. They are worn over a short boot or shoe and are fastened up the side by a variety of means such as leather loops, metal pins or laces, unlike the Spanish *polainas* which are fastened completely by leather loops and strap-type fastenings (that is, without any buckles or pins).

Hat

The hat (*chapéu*) is often one of the first things that takes a person's fancy when buying their first costume. There are various types and styles to choose from, one common style being the Mazzantini, an adaptation of the Spanish sombrero, but with buttons on the side of the crown, which has a ribbon running around the base.

The other most common hat has a wider, softer brim and the crown is not flat as the Mazzantini, but soft and indented, allowing it to follow the contour of the crown of the head. It is finished at the base of the crown with a ribbon that has a neat bow.

The most popular and correct hat colours for the rider are black, grey and brown. All brightly coloured hats are the reserve of the kiss-me-quick brigade.

As in Spain, it is normal to wear the hat tilted at an attractive angle, but I feel the brim should not be pulled down all the way round, which is a style often seen outside Portugal; this makes it look more like an English trilby.

Waistband

The finishing touch to the Portuguese outfit nowadays is a neatly tied waistband with the ends tucked in. As with the Spanish waistband, this is often a colourful headscarf rolled or folded to make a band just a few inches wide. This is more decorative than practical but without it the total effect is incomplete. In Portugal it is also common to see a waistband that fastens at the back, which is much more like a true cummerbund.

Portuguese women's costume

Much of the women's costume is the same in style as the men's, albeit not in cut. One option for the lady rider is the divided skirt, which allows the lady to ride astride, something women have not always been permitted to do.

The Hon. Lucinda Wynn riding her Lusitano gelding in a class at Windsor.

It is also usual for the ladies to wear often quite large, attractive earrings, some of the most intricate and delicate design, which would be frowned upon in Britain; earrings worn by Spanish lady riders are also supposed to be more discreet.

CAVALEIRO COSTUME

The *cavaleiro*'s choice of dress is a little more elaborate than that of the *rejoneador*. His colourful and richly embroidered satin frock coat covers a white frilly-fronted and cuffed white shirt that also sports a jabot, and his head is adorned by a cockaded tricorn hat. This is all reminiscent of the eighteenth century. The boots, the style of which is said to be of Napoleonic origin, come right up to the knee and are shaped to arch up the knee at each side of the leg; these boots are worn with breeches.

His horse is bedecked with ribbons running the full length of his majestic neck. They are carefully entwined in the tight double plaits of his mane, just like the Spanish running plaits.

The Portuguese School of Equestrian Art

A Escola Portuguesa de Arte Equestre, which was only established in the 1980s, is the pinnacle of classical riding in Portugal. Much of this school's work is possible thanks to a few dedicated and knowledgeable men such as Dr Guilherme Borba, who was also a guiding force in the early days of the Domecq School in Spain.

Whilst the riders are unpaid amateurs, they are extremely talented. Riding mainly the famous bay Alter Reals, they perform the most dramatic and elegant pieces from the classical school and are, in every way, the epitome of the bygone age they emulate. I first saw them performing in the mid-1980s at

A bay Lusitano stallion with his rider, Nuno Palma Santos, in the costume of the Portuguese School of Equestrian Art.

a British National Dressage Championships at Goodwood. It was wonderful to see such elegance and lightness amongst the somewhat tense competitive riding of that day.

The spectacle of colour they provide – brown, burgundy and gold – is only occasionally broken by the *Isabella*, the term used for the smaller, compact, cream, or coffee-coloured horse traditionally used for the airs above the ground. The School continues to perform regularly both in Portugal and on trips abroad, and a visit to one of their displays is highly recommended.

Chapter Nine

Training the Spanish Horse

I HAVE ALREADY STATED that 'dressage' simply means 'training', and so whatever you do with a horse, if he is being trained, he is being 'dressed'. The quality and the level of the dressage will vary depending on the horse, the trainer and the job to be done. I believe that all horses, no matter what path they will eventually follow, benefit from a good, basic classical training before branching out into their specific disciplines; this training will be outlined below.

Training a horse is about so much more than circles and straight lines, although these may be a good place to start. Fully understanding the art of training horses will take a lifetime and there are so many approaches to the training itself. Each rider will interpret concepts that have gone before, perhaps building on or adapting a method or a system to suit their own purpose; some will be good, some not so good. We are all different and consequently bring something different to the field of training.

Whilst this book looks at the subject of breaking and training in the context of Spanish and Lusitano horses and the particular fields in which they participate – *doma vaquera, doma clasica* – much of what is discussed is equally of benefit to competition dressage, as under FEI rules. It does not go into the general breaking and training process in great detail because this is much the same for all horses and is covered in a great many books.

Understanding Training

The Background

The breaking and training of any ridden horse is fundamentally the same today as it has been for centuries, and the basic training principles of the classical school are well proven. The systematic approach to classical training can be found in the writings of the great horsemen of our past: Xenophon, François Robichon de la Guérinière, François Baucher, James Fillis, Alois Podhajsky and Nuno Oliveira, to name but a few. Many may question the relevance of some of their work for modern-day competition dressage, but you cannot question the contribution these masters of equitation made to the development of horsemanship.

If we look at one or two of these masters briefly, it will show how much of their work is still influencing us today.

Xenophon (*c.* 430–354 BC) wrote a very early treatise, generally known as *The Art of Horsemanship*, covering the health, well-being and training of the horse. His approach was that of reward, kindness and caring, an approach that millennia later we still recognize and practise. There have been periods in between – the Dark Ages for example – when horse training was barbaric but, considering it was a time when people were subjected to various barbarous punishments, this would, no doubt, have been in keeping with the era.

François Robichon de la Guérinière (1688–1751) is believed to be the father of the shoulder-in, or shoulders-in depending on your view on angles. Guérinière stated that the shoulder-in was the alpha and omega of all exercises. His work was so profound and thorough that the Spanish Riding School in Vienna have subsequently based their training system on his ideas as outlined in *Ecole de Cavalerie* (*School of Horsemanship*).

In this book there are thorough descriptions of the airs above the ground including those two lesser known movements: the terre-à-terre and the mézair. The former, as mentioned earlier, is a two-beat form of canter on two tracks, when the horse raises both his front legs at the same instant and replaces them on the ground, again at the same instant. The hind legs follow the same action as the front. In effect it is a succession of small jumps, executed in a rocking-horse movement, that can be used to build up to the higher airs above the ground. As stated, in Guérinière's day it would have been performed on two tracks; today the terre-à-terre is seldom seen and when it is, for example at the Royal Andalusian School in Jerez, it is performed in a straight line, and usually within the sequence: piaffe, terre-à-terre and capriole.

Strictly, the mézair is a half air when, again, the forehand is elevated. It is a leap which, although included in the airs above the ground, is but a little higher than the terre-à-terre and was often referred to as a half-courbette. This describes it well because, unlike the full courbette, the forelegs return to the ground before the horse moves forward a short distance and the next mézair is performed. As with all classical movements like these, the picture must be graceful and when the legs are brought up, they must be held together. The mézair should be poised; not a stumble back into a rear with the forelegs flapping like a dog begging for a titbit, which describes the movement (purportedly a mézair) I once saw in a poor attempt to emulate a performance by The Spanish Riding School of Vienna.

François Baucher (1796–1873) was the first to perform the one-time changes, the change of leg at every canter stride, which ranks amongst the most difficult movements in dressage. He was also famous for his work in-hand; he was by no means the first to work a horse in-hand, but one of the best-known people at that time for his development of 'supplings'. His methods of suppling a horse from the ground, both at the halt and in movement, were then, and still are, a matter of controversy. He did prove without question, however, that the principles of his horsemanship were effective. It is well recorded that he had a number of the most difficult and dangerous mounts – some destined for the slaughterhouse – presented to him. After just eight to ten weeks he would perform high-school displays with these horses; an astounding feat, without doubt.

James Fillis (1834–1913), who became Ecuyer en Chef to the Cavalry School in Leningrad, had studied Baucher's methods under a pupil of Baucher's but later criticized some of Baucher's work, in particular his ideas on flexion. Interestingly, James Fillis went on to develop some new movements, none of which you will see in the competition dressage arena. Two of these were a canter on three legs and a Spanish trot-like movement, or polka as it is sometimes called, i.e. the raising of the forelegs every two strides. The foreleg action in the Spanish trot is similar to that of the Spanish walk, with the front legs raised to a high level. The hind legs must follow the trot rhythm and not move in walk time, as is often seen.

The Spanish trot should not be confused with the passage (particularly because at one time the passage was known as the Spanish trot). Today, the passage is understood to be the movement as required in the competition arena: a powerful, highly collected and very elevated development of trot, with a prolonged period of suspension in which the toe of the raised foreleg should reach approximately to the level of the middle of the cannon of the other foreleg, with the forearm of the raised leg ideally parallel to the ground. (The hind feet are not raised quite so high as the forefeet, but there should be equal elevation of both hind feet and both forefeet.)

In the Spanish trot, however, the horse stretches the front legs out at each stride as the hind legs thrust up and forward; the latter must each leave the ground in harmony with the front legs. Occasionally you will see this gait performed with the front legs swinging so high and irregularly that is impossible for the hind legs to leave the ground, and so the horse merely walks unevenly behind, which is not correct.

James Fillis also developed a considerable number of other movements. He claims to have created the canter in place and to the rear. To many, these would be somewhat bizarre exercises and would have no purpose in the dressage arena. However, I am sure that for a man like Fillis, these were purely means to develop and test his skills and control to the extreme.

Farolero, ridden by Peter Maddison-Greenwell, attempting his first few steps of Spanish trot.

The canter to the rear, when executed correctly, is the ultimate in lightness in the hand, as Nuno Oliveira could demonstrate. Whilst keeping the rhythm of the canter, the horse must retreat slowly. In the bullring, Alvaro Domecq would gallop his fantastic horse Opus backwards and forwards with great speed and control in front of a bull, taunting him to charge.

The canter in place has great worth in the training and execution of the pirouette. The rider must be able to hold the horse on the spot using the back and a light hand. The practice of holding the horse in collected canter in a straight line or on a circle for a number of strides is also excellent preparation for pirouettes.

One of the great lessons of James Fillis is on punishment. He said, 'Above all things a rider must not lose his temper.' He believed that when a horse deserved punishment it should be given, but that it must be 'proportionate to the offence'. He also maintained that if a horse disobeyed because of pain or discomfort, then the horse deserved understanding, not punishment.

There are also a great many excellent books by modern authors covering training from a straightforward, practical angle or looking at the subject from a more esoteric point of view. One of these authors was the above-mentioned Nuno Oliveira.

Oliveira (1925–1989) had intellect, academic training and talent, and was probably one of the last true exponents of the old school. He was often referred to as the Maestro, a title seldom used and less often justified. His books covered many aspects of classical training and riding, as well as the horse and the master/pupil relationship in a unique way. He gave us so many words of wisdom to contemplate, from the approach and attitude to the horse and the task in hand, to practical exercises when mounted. He talked about tact and finesse, and a lightness of hand *and* leg that many do not even consider. He was horrified by the abuse some 'dressage riders' would bestow upon their mounts. I found him inspirational and had the opportunity to watch him work, unfortunately only the once because shortly after this occasion he died; I am, however, fortunate to have a signed copy of his book *Reflections on Equestrian Art*. He is a great loss to horsemanship as I feel he was probably the modern gatekeeper of the classical art and few others will have so much to offer as this great man.

The Concept

For some people the word 'dressage' conjures up images of immaculately turned-out people riding impeccably turned-out horses around a white-bordered arena performing repetitive and seemingly complicated exercises, to prove that one person's horse can do said exercises better than other horses and thus deserves a rosette. This image still tends to prevail, even though many more people today understand that 'dressage' in its purest sense means to dress or train a horse for any field he may be required to work in. But do even those who know this really understand its principles, purposes, complexities and criteria?

The art of training horses can be a lifetime's uphill struggle, fraught with disappointment, frustration and physical and mental pain, and perhaps it takes a particular type of person to achieve the best results: someone who keeps an open mind, continues to search for knowledge, and who can be honest about their own ability and the errors they make. Arrogance and aggression have no place in the training of horses.

One such person who fits all the desired criteria is Delia Cunningham. Like many immensely intelligent and talented people she has unrelated and varied skills; she is an accomplished artist, musician and wind-surfer, and has held a position in the highest ranks of Britain's dressage competitors, having taken three horses to Grand Prix level. Now well past the age at which most people seek the comfort of the armchair, she continues to search for knowledge, to offer help and encouragement to others, and remains modest about her own ability and achievements, which are both many and great. Danielle and I owe her a great deal for her advice, knowledge, encouragement and, above all, her friendship. She was the first real dressage rider to take us and our work seriously.

Training horses should have a progressive and logical common-sense approach. It starts with the everyday handling of the horse and continues through to the development of particular abilities that are specific to the field in which the horse is to specialize. The stages in between include: introduction of equipment, lungeing, long-reining, in-hand work, backing, hacking, and flatwork. Some believe that there are short cuts that can be taken in this process, but remember, short cuts can have shortcomings.

My Training Methods

I can have twenty-five horses or more in my yard at any one time: some geldings, a few mares and sometimes more than thirteen stallions. We train our own horses for *doma vaquera*, *doma clasica* or high school; and some of them do a little of everything. We also train other people's horses for these disciplines, or simply for competition and/or pleasure riding. Whilst, for the last twenty years or so, I have concentrated on Spanish and Lusitano horses for myself, my methods of training all horses for all the disciplines are founded on what I believe to be good classical principles for a modern equestrian world and they are based on forty years broad-based experience of riding and training.

All of our horses must be able to fulfil a valuable and versatile role in life, for their own benefit and for that of their owners. A well-rounded education is of paramount importance and regardless of the quality or value of a horse, each should have a basic understanding of dressage movements, be able to jump a simple fence and ultimately be a pleasure to ride in the country either in company or alone. This 'foundation course' precedes the first year of concentrated school work. The old school called this initial training campaign riding, and it is well described in Alois Podhajsky's book, *The Complete Training of Horse and Rider*.

In the old days it was important that horses were trained to accept gun and cannon fire, flag waving, sword fighting, intense noise and shouting, people grabbing at their bridles, etc., which is far more than the average horse has to go through nowadays; but it is still required training for the cavalry horses and, in particular, those used for the mounted 'Skill at Arms' displays.

Our horses go through very similar training to prepare them for their shows, theatrical performances and corporate work. They must also be able to help open gates and work at close quarters and in confined spaces with others, regardless of gender. This training would also be given to many of our clients' horses when called for.

All the horses are well behaved in the stable and easy for any member of the team, male or female, to handle. Although I understand that some people believe in the notion that women should not handle stallions or wear perfume whilst with them, to date I have seen no evidence of this being a problem on our yard, whatever the breed of stallion. Perhaps we have been lucky, but I am more inclined to think it is down to good judgement, experience and attitude, not sex and smell. I do find, however, that Iberian stallions are sensitive to moods and attitudes and have noted that they will respond well to some handlers but will take advantage of others. These traits are not, of course, peculiar to Iberian horses, but are common amongst them.

An evenness of character and mood in the handler will be reflected in the horses, but aggression or nervousness promotes bad behaviour. Indeed, aggression is often a cover up for a handler's nervous disposition; it is well to remember, therefore, to be consistent and calm, and to learn about and

Farolero demonstrates his willingness to work happily whilst Peter Maddison-Greenwell carries a flag – exhibition at Olympia.

understand your horses in order to put yourself in the position of being able to trust them, and for them to trust you. This means being sensible and pragmatic when carrying out the everyday chores, such as tying up a horse to muck out or groom. When you know your horse really well, then you can afford to be a little more relaxed but, as with any relationship, do not take chances or take him for granted.

Once the good foundation has been laid, the specialist training can be started. The schooling requirements of *doma vaquera* will differ from those of competition dressage, which will differ again from those of high school and so on. We must not forget that not all horses and riders have the same natural ability or, for any number of reasons, will reach the same goal: we will not all be world champions or become members of The Spanish Riding School of Vienna. What is more important than the final result is the integrity in the work we produce, and the path we take in attaining that work.

The Basic System

Ideally, a horse should already be used to human contact and well handled by the time he reaches three to four years old (or by the time the breaking-in process begins). Handling at any age is good, as is leading and general socializing, but I believe it pays to be circumspect about when to start mounted work and the amount of hard lunge work given to young horses. Three to four years of age is a good general rule of thumb for most horses, but please remember that Spanish and Portuguese horses can mature as late as eight years of age and often do not finish growing and filling out until they are ten years old; and part-breds may mature more quickly than pure-breds depending on the cross (see Chapter 5).

Where possible I like to go through the basic education, including gentle hacking and a little school work when the horse is three, then turn him away until he's four before recommencing serious training; but even then, no regular, sustained fast and hard work should be given to Iberian horses until they have begun to mature.

Many people who have bred and reared their own horses or purchased youngstock may have tied up, groomed, led, rugged, boxed, socialized at shows, etc. by the time they come to start the riding process. If they have, it makes the whole job of training much easier, provided these things have been done well. Remember that horses, like children, are able to pick up and form bad habits far faster than they learn good ones. A horse who thinks he should be in charge, should do whatever he wants and go wherever he wants, is a disaster waiting to happen.

Communication

For young horses in the early stages of training, verbal or physical communication (aids) must be simple, clear and repeated as often as necessary. When young children learn to read they are presented with large letters, small words and short sentences. Similarly, with horses the advantage of the clear use of the voice and any physical aid at the beginning of training and working is obvious. As horses grow up and their education progresses, our communication with them must become ever more sophisticated and subtle. The seat, hand and leg aids are laid over one another in a variety of combinations to effect, for example, transitions between piaffe and passage in quick succession, or pirouette to tempi changes to pirouette. It must be remembered however, that verbal aids, so useful when training or working, are not allowed in dressage competitions.

The Breaking Process

This is a vitally important stage in a horse's training and it must be done with care, patience and understanding. With this in mind, although it is an expedient phrase that encompasses more than just 'backing', 'breaking-in' is perhaps an unfortunate term for this practice, as it suggests a somewhat harsh and crude method for the first stages in the education of a young horse – and it need not be like this. Nevertheless it should be a time when discipline and manners are well and truly instilled, particularly if they are not there already. Fundamentally, the principles of the basic education are the same whatever the end aim: an acceptance of the bit and rider, a sound steering system and, above all, good brakes. Moving is essential but the ability to stop is vitally important. To this end I place a lot of emphasis on stopping and standing still very early.

A good common-sense approach to building confidence steadily is by far the best method. Asking for just a little at a time, going from lungeing to long-reining to mounting in a way that is progressive and free from tension and nervousness for all concerned should make the process a pleasure and not a battle. There are always going to be differences of opinion between you and your charge and you must be sure that what you are asking is fair and reasonable before any punishment is meted out. I, like James Fillis, do feel that punishment is occasionally necessary, but it must always be in balance with reward; too much of either one without the other will spoil the horse. If you do find yourself in conflict with your horse, you must see it through, in other words, do not rattle the cage if you are not prepared to go in and sort out the problem.

If all is relatively straightforward, the initial process leading up to mounting could take around four to six weeks. Never be in a rush to get on the horse; he needs muscle and balance if he is to carry a rider comfortably and willingly. I see little or no point in any rider risking their health, and the horse's confidence, by suddenly leaping on and riding out the bucks and antics that so often follow this short cut.

In all the years I have been breaking horses – and I have broken many – I have only ever had one horse I started myself attempt to throw his rider. I may have spoken too soon here, but I think you will appreciate the point. A horse who wishes to dump you at any given excuse is no fun and can cause major clashes. It is, therefore, important to establish a training precedent: I achieve a willingness to accept a rider by gradually increasing the horse's experience, from a little slap of the saddle and a pull on the stirrup to the rider actually lying across the horse's back. I take no risks and end every lesson on a good note.

Only experience and common sense will tell you how far to go in each step. The whites of the horse's eyes and the agitated fidgeting should give you a clue as to whether you have gone too far, too fast. It is imperative that those taking part in the backing session must be calm and quiet; slow and positive in their actions, but quick in their reactions. This is not a job for the beginner or an aggressive or nervous person; if you fit these categories, find proven, experienced and knowledgeable help – it's worth every penny you might have to pay them not to risk ending up in hospital or ruining the rest of your horse's life.

As stated earlier, it is not this book's intention to give a step-by-step account of breaking-in, but I would refer readers to the books listed in Recommended Reading at the end of this book.

In-hand and Mounted Work

On the ground, the way you position your body and the general body language are both effective and essential for building up a sound foundation on which to base future schooling. When you lunge you place yourself in front of the horse's shoulder to slow or halt him, and behind the shoulder to move the horse forwards. When we begin work in-hand we again place ourselves in positions to move our horse forwards, sideways, backwards or halt to best effect. For example, whilst initiating the first few steps in the turn on the forehand, we take the inside rein and flex the horse slightly to the inside with one hand whilst placing our other hand (or, indeed, the whip used as an extension of our arm) to touch the horse on the ribs or the flank to effect one step at a time, following through with the body and keeping up with each movement. This is purely the first step; once the horse understands the process, the outside rein should be picked up and used to avoid a twisting of the head or neck.

Although work in-hand is still quite rare in Britain, it is an immensely valuable training method by which many movements can be taught at walk before the horse is expected to perform the same movements under saddle with the added problem of having to carry a rider. At the simplest level, I find it quite natural when lungeing to then ask the horse to take a few steps sideways away from me. By way of progression, a leg-yield from the centre line to the wall, a turn on the forehand, or a shoulder-in on a circle, all performed simply through the use of a *serreta* or cavesson, the positioning of the trainer and subtle signals from the whip, are exercises that can prove to be of great benefit later on when the horse's schooling progresses.

Working this way not only gives you the opportunity to observe how your horse is moving but also, most importantly, prepares the horse to accept the whip as an aid without fear. If the horse accepts the trainer positioned at his haunches using the whip correctly on the quarters or legs at this stage, the lesson will not have to be learned later in the horse's training when more advanced movements, particularly piaffe and passage, are being taught. I have attended clinics (even at the highest level) where all too often horses show fear of the whip and even kick out or rear, forcing the trainer to take evasive action. This can be avoided so easily with careful preparation in-hand.

In-hand work is worthy of a book in its own right but an excellent reference source for the subject is Nuno Oliveira's *Reflections on Equestrian Art*.

When you are ready to mount the young horse, even if you are to be in the saddle for only a brief time, ensure that the horse is given the reward of a gentle stroke and a kind word; and, once you are in the saddle, ask the horse for just a few steps a day for the first few days, with the horse under close control from a trusted colleague on the ground. Every moment of calm, relaxed movement is setting the standard for the future. These first few steps will soon lead to your horse working safely on the lunge under a rider, until he is performing all three basic gaits in a happy, relaxed and forward manner on both reins.

At this point a judgement based on experience must be made. If the horse is kept on the lunge for a few days, the person lungeing is in a position to control the horse if it becomes necessary for the rider to quit the saddle. However, there is the potential risk of the horse rearing, spinning round and wrapping the lunge line around the rider. This should obviously be avoided at all costs. Alternatively, some people prefer to leave the horse and rider free once the rider is in the saddle. Either method has its risks. I would hope that by the time the horse is ready to be mounted, the trainer has the measure of the horse's temperament and chooses the way to progress wisely and carefully.

At this stage, a relatively small enclosed environment with good footing and no distractions is ideal and safest for all concerned and, certainly in the all-important early days, picking the right time for a horse to take those first steps under saddle is crucial. A wise move is to work in the early morning or later in the evening when everyone has gone home, leaving just you, your horse and an assistant in peace.

There is nothing worse than having just settled yourself on a young colt, when a well-meaning member of staff lets your mares out into a nearby field or a visitor parks by the manège, drops their trailer ramp loudly and starts to unload the animal within. With stallions in particular, I spend a lot of time in the manège during the early schooling, preferring to hack out once I feel I can trust the horse to stay under control regardless of what we are likely to meet. Falling off or coming down with a stallion who becomes uncontrollable for whatever reason, especially through no fault of his own, is a horrendous situation. A loose horse in today's traffic is one of the most frightening and dangerous scenarios you can think of.

For about the last twenty years I have always been lucky enough to have the facilities of a school, direct access into countryside and relatively quiet lanes, giving me the opportunity to expose a horse to all the new sights and sounds of today's busy world gradually. The presence of an old and trusted horse will help to steady a youngster and even provide shelter from passing traffic, monster dustbins and prams accelerating rapidly out of gateways. Modern campaign-riding experience is provided by the roar of high-speed cars, towering billboards, bus shelters and noisy crowds.

Whilst it is desirable that a young horse is good in company, whatever the gender of the companion horse, it is equally important that he will go out on his own and not nap back towards the yard or his chums. As soon as is feasible, I spend a lot of time long-reining up and down the lanes and in the fields, taking advantage of all obstacles, natural and otherwise, to go round, over or in and out. A horse makes light work of these things if he does not have to think additionally about balancing a rider, and he will also be used to all these things by the time he carries a rider.

The trainer guides and controls the horse by walking a safe distance behind him with one of the long-reins in each hand. There are a variety of methods of long-reining, and Sylvia Stanier's excellent book *The Art of Long Reining* describes them simply and clearly. The method I favour is to have the horse saddled and I run the reins under the stirrups and over the saddle. The stirrups should be adjusted to an average leg length and connected to each other under the horse's belly; an old stirrup leather is ideal for this. Strapping the stirrups together prevents them from banging against the horse's sides as he moves, and stops them from flipping up over the saddle should the horse rear or jump about if things get a little fraught.

Whilst it is unlikely that you will meet everything that could conceivably upset a young horse in these early stages, by introducing your horse to whatever you do meet calmly and by never asking too much of him, you will ensure that generally the lessons are stress free and end in success. It is your horse's ability to approach any challenge without fear of punishment for failure that makes each new task achievable and establishes an attitude of co-operation, willingness and confidence.

Good Manners

People often say that you should never trust a yard-reared horse, and certainly youngsters reared in a natural herd environment will at least be taught the social graces and respect for others, if only for other horses, by their peers. But keeping a herd is not always possible, particularly in England where most breeders only breed a small number of horses a year and do not have the vast expanses of land available to the large studs in Spain, Portugal and the Americas.

One major issue with young horses, particularly colts, is that of biting. This often becomes apparent only when the handling and breaking process begins, as you are then in close contact with a youngster for longer and the temptation for him to nip or bite is irresistible. You can be bitten anywhere, but the bottom is always a good target when you are picking up the youngster's feet, or saddling up. Young horses will nip and bite each other in the herd as a form of play, seldom maliciously or with any truly bad intent, but they are also testing where their boundaries lie with their peers. They are, therefore, really only doing the same with a human handler, but even a gentle bite will be more painful to a human than to another horse.

My advice is that prevention is better than cure. Make sure that the youngster is taught to tie up as early as possible, so that the head can at least be controlled in situations when biting might occur. Use a sharp tone to tell the horse off, but only punish the horse if it is really necessary. If you are firm and consistent in the way you deal with biting, the youngster will soon desist. All young stallions are inclined to experiment with their mouths and teeth but, with good guidance, will grow out of it. It should also be borne in mind that when you are dealing with foals, they, like other baby animals, may have uncomfortable gums as their first teeth are breaking through and might decide to use you as a teething aid.

One particularly dangerous form of biting is breast biting; I know of a number of women who have had serious injuries to the breast as a direct outcome of this. A horse who bites is not going to differentiate between the more vulnerable parts of the human body and other less delicate areas. A bite to the breast normally occurs because women tend to like to cuddle their horses and generally place their bodies too close to the horse's head. Constantly fiddling and fussing in this area is not necessary and is not the same as grooming and building a relationship where your horse accepts your touch. A kind voice and a gentle stroke of the neck are just as rewarding and far safer. Unfortunately, in many cases this inappropriate approach to stallions, or indeed many other horses, encourages what might be considered a kind of play to begin with, but it can soon lead to a painful and often dangerous outcome.

Spanish horses and Lusitanos are known for their good temperaments (see Chapter 5) and it is very rare to see one bite or kick, but this does not mean that it will never happen; always be aware of what you are doing when handling all horses.

Good manners are the foundation stones of any horse's education. Even if the horse does not have the talent or conformation you would wish for, if he has good manners he will always be a pleasure to be with; you and your horse will be welcome everywhere and you will be envied by many.

How Does Your Horse Respond to You?

Why is it that we see some people struggling to get their horse to listen to them whilst others get immediate attention, when it is not apparent that they are doing anything differently? The answer is that it is not so much what we do, but how we do it! The way in which we treat our horses reflects what we believe about ourselves and the way in which we interact with others. There are direct comparisons in the way we behave with our horses, our relatives, friends and colleagues; our approach, our posture, our body language, our tone of voice, our patterns of behaviour are all a part of our communication with others and, in particular, our horses.

We use our sensitive Spanish and Lusitano stallions as a part of an ever-evolving developmental course helping people with their personal and organizational skills. We can situate people in what we call 'a sacred place' where, by spending time alone with a horse it will soon become apparent that there can be no lies, no deceit, only a true reflection of yourself, your intentions and thus your possibilities.

Horses are not impressed by the latest designer labels, the top-of-the-range executive motor or even the biggest salary in the management team. They only respond to that which is truly harboured within, whether it be good or evil. You cannot lie to a horse. You cannot pretend honesty, or gloss over, skirt round or disguise ill-intent, negativity, anger, selfishness or any of the other disruptive emotions that get in the way of a strong bond between two beings: the kind of bond that drives men to follow a great warrior into battle, despite mental and physical exhaustion, pain and fear, or that inspires sports teams to give their absolute all to achieve a world championship, or a company's workforce to go beyond the nine-to-five attitude and become successful, well-respected and to keep their team together.

To create that kind of authentic relationship with any other being demands a greater depth of self-knowledge, confidence and belief than is found in most modern corporations today. If you are not completely aligned and resolute in what you believe, the horse will find you out, no matter what it says on your business card or how many people appear to bow and scrape to your job title.

Here we get into the realms of positive thought and inner energy. It is what makes some people lead effortlessly and others follow. For many, this may just be the difference between success and failure with their horses. You know how to do something, you have been taught and appear to be going about things the right way but, no matter how hard you try, your horse just doesn't try with you.

Let me give you an example by telling you about two men on one of our developmental and confidence-building courses. One stood over 1.8 m (6 ft) tall and weighed 95 kg (210 lb) or more. The other man was 1.7 m (5 ft 6 in) tall and weighed considerably less. Neither had any previous experience with horses and both had been given the same simple task of moving the same horse sideways in-hand. The first man, having had a number of attempts and achieving only one step, gave up. The second, smaller, man had several attempts and succeeded. What was the difference? Neither of them could tell why the one man succeeded, or could say what each had done differently from the other, nor could the other members of the group.

They both followed the technique given them almost to the letter; the only difference between them was their individual natures or temperaments. The first man had the advantage of stature but the second man more than made up for his smaller size with his energy. He was a bubbly, charismatic, larger-than-life man who wanted only to get on and succeed; he saw no challenge as too much and no handicap in being shorter and smaller than the first man.

The first man, although physically big and strong, was quiet and unassuming, even a little weak in attitude, hence giving up so soon. He stood with rounded shoulders and his hands in his pockets most of the time, and walked and moved slowly without any energy. I playfully but firmly jabbed him in the small of his back with two fingers, one either side of his backbone, thus making him immediately lift his chest and take a sharp intake of breath. In consequence he stood taller, with his chest thrust out, and considerably more alert. With this different stance he tried to move the horse sideways again; this time the result was successful and the horse moved willingly.

This was a simple lesson to prove that we need to use positioning, stature, and posture to make the most of ourselves in order to achieve the desired effect and succeed.

One delegate gave us some interesting feedback:

> On reflection the two days for me were about making decisions and the fact that this can be a barrier to learning in itself. Taking action, being influenced, and at times delayed, by the inner dialogue of self-doubt, self-confidence and risk assessment. A learning that hesitation can sometimes lead to a decision being taken out of your hands or someone else taking control (in my case a horse running off across an arena because I had a split second's doubt about my ability).

> The decision: I can do this vs I can't do this/I will do this vs I won't do this. It's about choice.

> Having looked back through my personal notebook a few days later I was surprised not only by what I had captured, but also by just how much I had written and therefore had learnt. This has turned out to be even more than I was probably aware of at the time.

Another part of creating an understanding between you and your horse is your approach: who is in charge? It is imperative that your horse appreciates that you are the driver, the one in charge, the leader, and this can only be the result of trust and respect – neither of which will be achieved by force alone. I say 'force alone' as it is surely true that a ballet dancer will not perform her best work at gunpoint, and no horse will give his all if he is constantly in fear of the whip or spur.

Punishment

It is popular in some circles to advocate the so-called 'gentle approach' and to never chastise, never carry a whip or use the spur. Advocates of this policy are misguided in their belief that this is the 'classical approach'. It may be that for some horses and people this might just work, but for the majority it is a balance of frequent praise, reward and occasional punishment. Horses, like children, feel safer and more confident when they have clear boundaries that are applied kindly and consistently. This sometimes means that when a horse steps over that boundary, he has to be helped to understand that this behaviour is not acceptable.

'Punishment' is perhaps an emotive word, and it must be emphasized that my approach is not about anger or viciousness; it is about assertiveness, tenacity and determination, always tempered within a relationship by respect and love for the animal. Most people who have lived and worked with working animals understand this well and it is merely common sense to them. The punishment must always fit the crime and go no further.

In my opinion, punishment is generally applied in the teaching of manners: correcting kicking, biting, barging and so on. Once these problems have been corrected in the early stages of training in-hand, in the stable and whilst riding, punishment as such is seldom necessary in the actual teaching of dressage.

Under saddle, the whip is used to support the leg if the horse chooses to ignore the leg aid for forward or sideways movement. It is used by the rider in the piaffe and passage to encourage a hind leg to step under more, by a touch on the lower hind leg or even near the hock; by a quick flick of the wrist the rider can call the horse to attention without moving the hand. The whip is also used by the trainer teaching piaffe and passage from the ground by applying it lightly on, below or above the hocks, or on the side of the quarters. Only experienced trainers should do this because it can have grave consequences if the horse has not been prepared properly to accept the whip: he may kick out, turn round on you, swing his quarters out or even rear, as discussed earlier.

It must be understood that any work like this with the whip *must not* be seen as punishment by either human or horse. The horse must not be intimidated by the whip and become tense or uncontrollably excited, which is counter-productive. The more sensitive the horse, the more tactful and patient you must be.

Consistency in punishment is essential. It is no good punishing for something trivial one day and letting something serious go without consequence the next. Let me give you an all-too-common dog-owner problem as an example.

If you always allow your dogs to jump on the furniture because it is old and has seen better days, you cannot get angry and punish them for coming in from a walk covered in mud and jumping on the new, very expensive, white leather sofa you have just purchased. If you do, the dogs will be confused and upset, and it will be your fault.

Similarly, if you let your horse walk off every time you mount, the day he walks off and you fall off the mounting block and under the horse, still hung up by your left leg, it's *your* fault, but this time *you* will be confused.

Reward

We all like to think we know enough about reward, but is that really true? I know that the more I learn (one good consequence of ageing), the more I find myself rewarding more and punishing less. I only wish I had learnt this much earlier and can honestly say I have made mistakes in the past.

I now find myself telling my pupils that they must have patience and give their horses a chance; they cannot give more than they are capable of at a particular time: they might not be strong or supple enough yet, etc.

More is achieved with a break in the work, a short rest and a comforting stroke or kind word than with the punishing repetition of strenuous work under pressure of spur and threat of stick. The more you grit your teeth and demand it, and the tenser you get, the less you and your horse are able to achieve.

Reward and praise does not mean stopping to give titbits, over-expressive hugs and kisses or loud, highly excited squeaks just because your horse has stopped square for once. This is unnecessary and often disruptive.

Rewarding is recognizing the moment when extra effort or a small but symbolic change of attitude in work is made, or an extra step in the right direction in new movements. Knowing your horse's character and temperament will tell you the appropriate moment and the amount to praise. For some, a light touch of the hand the instant an achievement is noted is enough. For others, a stop, a lowering of the neck and a good stroke accompanied with some kind words will do the job better.

With excitable or nervous horses it is not wise, for example, to drop a rein and put your hand forwards up the neck to caress immediately after a flying change, as this can lead to a surge forward and a loss of concentration and balance, thus defeating the object of keeping a steady contact through a difficult moment. It is often better to go a few more strides in the canter, come down to walk and then drop the rein and praise.

Most horses, in particular the Spanish and Lusitano, are social beings and want to be appreciated. At the end of a lesson they, like people, want to know that they have done well. It may not all have been good, but a wise trainer seeks to end on a successful note, finishing as friends and saying 'thank you' by caressing the horse's neck, giving some sugar, or a horse nut or mint treat, and putting the horse away happy.

I like to always end the lesson in the centre of the arena on a loose rein; to stand for a short while perfectly still. I dismount, loosen the girth, loosen the curb, praise the horse and lead him quietly back to the stables.

Having established that punishment and reward must be given in fair proportion, it is important to realize that this is only a part of what makes a leader. Other good leadership qualities include fairness, consistency, decisiveness and, above all, respect; the giving of respect should in turn generate respect. By following these guidelines in life you will achieve more from your chosen equine partner – and perhaps others you meet, too.

General Training Pointers

When training for *doma vaquera*, *doma clasica* and competition dressage, there are certain points that are specific to each field, but a great many of the training methods can apply across the board; I shall deal with those first.

Owing to these breeds' more elevated action, Spanish and Lusitano horses need to have their walk worked on. Too often they are allowed to walk with a hollow back, taking short steps behind and not tracking up. A good dressage horse must be able to raise his back and walk through if he is to develop the strength and flexibility to sustain long-term soundness and to achieve the more advanced work correctly.

On the other hand, the majority of these horses perform what is generally considered advanced work with more ease than other breeds; they have no problems with piaffe and passage, for example, because they find it easier to collect than extend. They can spin on a sixpence, piaffe for fun without any training, and can stand on their hind legs for as long as it takes you to make a cup of tea.

This natural ability to collect occasionally attracts the type of owner who hopes to be able to perform piaffe, passage, pirouettes and Spanish walk with no foundation work. Despite the skills inherent in these breeds, the movements must be developed correctly. The temptation to start any of these movements too soon, without any previous experience or sound knowledge of how they should be done (or even the correct criteria for each movement), presents countless problems to such owners and, more importantly, their horses.

Cases in point are the Spanish walk and the levade or pesade. There are a number of books that will either give the method of how to begin these movements or, perhaps, how to ride them, but they do not necessarily give the whole picture, or explain what stage of a horse's training they should be taught.

Peter Maddison-Greenwell riding two horses in piaffe: ABOVE LEFT *Farolero;* ABOVE RIGHT *Florence Hunt's Batanero.*

The Spanish walk is one of the most difficult movements to teach and is of the same level as piaffe, so should not be taught until a horse is at an advanced level of training. There are two reasons for this. First, you should not teach a horse to strike out with his front legs at an early age; this is not a weapon you want to hand to an unruly youth. Second, a major criterion of this movement is that the horse should step through from behind with regular strides. A good basic walk must therefore be established before the Spanish walk is taught. Serious dressage trainers from certain schools frown on this movement as they say it flattens the back and is not natural. It will undoubtedly flatten the back if it is taught before a horse is strong and walks correctly but, regarding the nature of the movement, it is one of the most natural things for a stallion in particular to do. You only have to observe the action of young colts at liberty together, or that of a stallion either in a herd with his mares or waiting impatiently for dinner. Nuno Oliveira stated that this 'walk in suspension' can be of great help in developing freedom in the shoulder.

The levade, or its close relative the pesade, may be what an inexperienced rider is hoping to achieve, but the end result is almost always an undisciplined rear. Both these airs above the ground are high-school movements and, like the Spanish walk, should only be taught when the horse is at an advanced level of training. These movements have specific criteria: they require the ultimate

Peter Maddison-Greenwell riding the bay Tres Sangres stallion, Saeta, and the grey Pure-bred, Farolero, in Spanish walk. The reason for riding the movement with the reins in one hand becomes apparent when the garrocha is carried.

in collection, control and balance as well as considerable strength; the pesade should be performed at an angle of approximately 45 degrees to the ground, and the levade at a lesser angle.

If, as a result of starting this work too soon, the horse starts to rear, he will often use this as a resistance and then learn to go higher and higher until the rider is unseated or unnerved.

I am afraid that I have spent a lot of time giving warnings such as these both in this book and in my everyday work, but they are based on experience: things I have learnt myself through observation and the sound advice of others. I have no desire to clip the wings of people wishing to experiment and learn, but only to point out that so many problems, and even disasters, can be avoided with a little less haste and a little more thought and well-founded knowledge.

Horses Need Help

There is no such thing as the perfect horse, although for half a million pounds or more you can get pretty close to perfection. It is unbelievable how much a dressage horse can change hands for in this day and age and it is, therefore, no wonder that some people become so disillusioned and frustrated when they realize they just can't afford to compete on the same playing field.

If you can forget the actual value of the horse and simply concentrate on what it is that makes one horse more valuable in a trainer's or rider's eyes, you will see that there are a number of qualities that make up the as-near-perfect-as-possible horse. In no particular order they are: good temperament, presence, strong and well-proportioned conformation, straight, balanced, fluid, regular and big movement, ample stamina, suppleness, agility and, above all, intelligence. With Spanish and Lusitano horses, the outstanding looks are a bonus.

If you consider that you need all of these ingredients in abundance to excel in competition you will realize that finding them in one package is not going to be easy and, in most cases, one or more shortcomings must be accepted. Also, generally speaking, the lower the budget, the greater the short-fall. Do not, however, despair: if you are honest and realistic about the shortcomings, many can be resolved, or certainly improved, with understanding, patience and good training.

The following issues may appear to be addressed primarily from a 'dressage' point of view but, bearing in mind that dressage is simply a word for training, you will see that they are pertinent to the training of any horse.

BACKS

We have previously discussed the subject of weakness in the back, which is dictated to a greater or lesser degree by the back being dipped; the most severe presentation of which is the sway back. Some horses have straight or even slightly arched backs which can more easily support weight, although the particular conformational extreme of this, the roach back, is neither attractive nor comfortable. A roach back bows upward from the withers and appears to drop down into the quarters rather than flow into them in a smooth line.

Weak backs require a lot of attention to ensure that they are encouraged to come up under the saddle, initiated by the lowering of the neck and the propulsion from the hind legs. The other way to help weak-backed horses is to give them plenty of exercise climbing progressively steeper hills at walk and eventually at trot and canter. Furthermore, going to the top of a hill means that you have to come down again, and this helps a horse to lower his neck and haunches and flex the hocks, promoted by the forward momentum of his own weight, thus encouraging the horse to step further under his body than he would normally do on the flat.

Another good exercise to do on the hill is to place the horse in shoulder-in. As he goes uphill this loads more weight onto the haunches; the effect has the same principle as someone working in the gym with heavier weights than usual. As with all remedial or fitness and muscular development work, it must be taken slowly and progressively and the horse must be given frequent breaks. I cannot emphasize this enough. You know how easy it is to overdo exercise and be stiff, or even bedridden, for the next day or two.

Long backs are more common in mares and whilst they are good for brood mares, giving a developing foal plenty of room, they can be too weak for dressage. Despite this drawback, a long back will feel comfortable, owing to the fact that the back acts a little like a suspension bridge, giving at each stride.

Iberian horses tend to have short backs and, if you are lucky, the back will also slope slightly 'uphill' to the neck, which is the right combination for an impressive piaffe, because such horses can lower the haunches with greater ease. Too short a back, however, can give a harsh ride because it tends to throw the rider upwards – the opposite effect of the long back.

Horses who are short-coupled do tend to find most work simple, especially the more advanced work. They find it easy to turn in the pirouettes, spring forwards from walk to canter, etc. because lowering the quarters and carrying the forehand is made less of a task by the geometry of their conformation. They can, however, find bending and flexing more difficult owing to the body being shorter and 'tighter'. Therefore these horses need ample time spent on suppling.

Riding shoulder-in frequently will supple and stretch the muscles laterally as well as flexing the horse through his whole body. To give extra flexion of the neck, use an opening rein in a soft, encouraging way. Do not pull the inside rein backwards, which tends to compress the neck and twist the head if insufficient support is given by the outside hand; this incorrect use of the reins in shoulder-in is a common fault of many riders. A good suppling exercise for short-backed horses is shoulder-in to renvers to shoulder-out to travers, based both on a straight line and a circle. Counter-canter, ridden correctly, also has a suppling role. Developing a good suppling routine that works for you and your horse is a good way to start a schooling session, and far more productive than asking new and difficult movements of him whilst he is still stiff.

NARROW CHESTS

For those horses with narrow chests, any form of lateral work, crossing and stretching the forelegs, will help develop the chest and shoulders. Quarter

A shoulder-in ridden with expression and correct aiding – note rider's heel well down and inside leg on the girth. The horse is the Yeguada Susaeta's Macanuo.

turns on the haunches in a square progressing to pirouettes in the walk all help develop the chest area in the same way.

One useful tip particularly for a young colt – although I see no reason why it cannot benefit any horse – is to tie him up before meal times, and to feed the other horses before him. Whilst he is waiting for his supper he will stand to attention. This will also teach him a certain amount of patience, which is character-building and good for discipline; although some horses might fidget whilst waiting, it is still good discipline. Even when he is used to the routine and stands quietly he will still stand tall and strong, which in itself will put on muscle. The action of lifting the head and standing proudly tends to make Spanish horses 'puff out their chests'.

Quarters

Some Iberian horses suffer from weak quarters, a problem that demands a great deal of work to get the horses stepping under and through. You cannot ignore the hind end, it is the engine, the driving force, the part that propels the horse forwards and upwards, without which you are forever earthbound. This point is discussed further in the next section, Energy and Strength. As with backs, hill work will put muscle on the quarters, such preparation being necessary before any serious demands are made of the horse.

Energy and strength

Spanish and Lusitano stallions who are weak in the quarters can still give the impression of being strong because of their vivacious nature, agility and heart; nevertheless this is not enough if you are to compete at a serious level. This energy must be put to good use to develop muscle in the right places. Sometimes these stallions will fool you by sheer testosterone power. At a point where other horses give up, a good stallion will dig deeper and draw on amazing reserves, which can be harnessed for good use. (But if a stallion should use the energy against you, you realize that, just when you think you have got to the bottom of the well, and perhaps he will now relax, give in and give you what you want, he finds even more energy!)

This kind of energy is fantastic. It is stimulated by pride when another stallion or gelding enters the arena, or by sexual attraction if a mare comes within range. Sometimes the excitement becomes so intense that relaxation becomes impossible and, when the blood is up, it is not easily settled. When this trait is understood and harnessed it can be of great benefit, producing, for example, really expressive movements like piaffe and passage. But this is just energy and is not the strength it purports to be; the strength you need for such controlled work as the classical pirouettes when the horse moves in a slow rhythm and carries both his and your weight on his lowered haunches. In a movement like this the horse cannot just substitute energy or speed for strength because the movement will be rushed or simply collapse before it is complete. (The situation is slightly different for the rapid *vaquera* pirouettes – in these, whilst both energy and strength are highly desirable, there is more reliance upon sheer momentum than is the case with the classical form.)

If the quarters are weak it is almost impossible to sustain advanced movements with rhythm and control and if pirouettes are attempted too soon with weak hindquarters even the pelvis can suffer and the long, arduous task of remedial work is required.

The advanced movements themselves will, of course, build the muscles if performed correctly, but before you get to them you must prepare with less demanding work. As that is what dressage is all about, this may seem like an obvious statement, but I cannot re-emphasize these points too often. School exercises are essential, from something as simple as varying the trot – moving forward from a smaller trot to a bigger trot – to the more advanced walk to canter, and canter to halt to rein-back to canter.

Young Spanish horses can have shortcomings, as can any breed, but with wise, steady work it is amazing how they can develop and mature way beyond our wildest dreams, as long as they are treated well.

STRAIGHTNESS

It is commonly understood that most horses have a soft and a hard side. When going in a straight line they may be heavier in one hand than the other; in particular, it is common that circling to the right requires more effort than to the left. This is quite normal and there are various theories put forward to explain it. It may be, for example, that most people are right-handed and do not take care to lunge evenly, preferring to carry the lunge whip in their right hand and do more circles to the left, thus starting the horse on the path to being more flexible to the left. It is, therefore, important to change direction frequently and to study the horse's movement to check whether he is well able to track up to the same degree in each direction. If it is obvious that he finds working to the left easier, you should start and finish the lunge session on the right rein, thus doing more on the difficult side.

When the horse is working under saddle, it is essential that he remains straight and works evenly, i.e. everything must be taught and performed equally to the left and the right. Every stride must have the same length and propulsion for each aspect of the walk, trot and canter. As training becomes more advanced this becomes more relevant and if the matter of correctness in the basic work is not dealt with in the earlier stages you will be forever struggling to advance to the next level.

Remedial work

Sometimes, in various ways and for various reasons, horses are acquired who require a great deal of remedial work to get them back, physically and mentally, onto the right track. Although this can be very demanding work, it can also be very educational and rewarding – and a positive result is pretty strong evidence that one's training philosophy is on the right track. On the other hand, 'remedial work' that involves coercive methods and attempts at 'quick fixes' will usually backfire spectacularly, to the further detriment of the horse. The following is an example of a successful, albeit protracted, retrieval.

I had a horse brought to me some years ago with a bad attitude to work and she was the worst stargazer I had seen. The owner proudly told me she had broken the horse herself and now wanted the horse to learn dressage.

On watching the owner ride I was astounded by how badly she rode. Her hands pulled and jarred the horse so much in an attempt to maintain her own balance it was heartbreaking. There was no intention to hurt the horse; the owner simply had no idea of her own lack of knowledge and ability. The poor mare was by now well and truly damaged mentally and physically. After I had made several attempts to school the horse and rider together, the owner had the good grace to acknowledge her shortcomings and gave up. Sadly, it was just a bad combination: the owner's inexperience, lack of natural ability and absolutely no understanding of what was required to break and school any horse – let alone a sensitive horse with some quality.

Subsequently, the horse was given to us but it took a year to nurse her through her emotional problems and tantrums, which I truly believe were caused by ignorance and clumsy handling. The mare would do so much then throw herself down on the ground in a fit of pique rather than perform a simple task. Being spoilt had made her want her own way to the point of blind rage when she did not get it, and the rider's constant banging down on her back and harsh jerking of the bit had caused her obvious pain over a long period, which resulted in a difficult, unruly and totally misunderstood horse.

We overcame this by turning her out with other mares in an attempt to clear her mind and calm her. She was kept out all summer and for safety reasons was given no hard food and kept unshod. She was then slowly and steadily retrained from the very beginning. It was a case of one step forwards and two steps back on many occasions, but with a firm yet understanding approach we eventually brought her round.

She was given lots of lungeing and long-reining work to bring her head and neck down and her back up, then we slowly introduced a rider as if she were being backed for the first time. Even with this careful approach she still had moments of anxiety when she would nap and attempt to bolt. We worked very much on the principle of little and often, and every spell of good work, no matter how short, was praised, and work was stopped on a positive note before a negative incident occurred.

After the year's work she became happy and well-balanced and is proving to be a pleasurable and useful horse for her new owners, to whom she was sold at a reasonable price. From a commercial point of view, the price attained would never have justified the work put into the horse, and this is the dilemma for many. The commercial cost of professional help far outweighs the value of many horses and so often exceeds the budgets of those who struggle to keep their horses in the first place, forcing many to either give up or take free advice from ill-informed, but probably well-meaning, people.

Fortunately for many, there are horses out there who will endure such appalling riding and bad treatment, but sadly you can often see the misery reflected in their eyes. This happens throughout the horse world, not just the Spanish and Lusitano horse community, when some people will do almost anything to own their dream horse, but then realize that they have taken on more than they can handle and the dream turns into a nightmare.

Back to Basics

To go back to basics and to lay firm foundations for the future, there are two methods that can be used, both of which will be of benefit in a horse's development: 'deep and round' or 'long and low'.

As I understand it, some trainers advocate one method, whilst some advocate the other. These techniques have both had their day in the sun, with one technique being more fashionable than the other at some stage. They are often featured in magazines with the techniques' disciples saying that we should only do 'A' now and not 'B'. I feel that they both have their place because, if the horse is ridden so that the hind legs step well under the body, they will both bring the horse's back up and be of benefit in their own way.

DEEP AND ROUND

There are horses who are particularly sensitive and, perhaps, of a nervous disposition, and they can be especially energetic or, as we say 'hot'. These horses might need to be brought between hand and leg right from the start for the purpose of control, and riding them deep and round for a short period will help to dominate them. I use the word 'dominate' with care because it can imply the use of unnecessary force. My method is to put the horse 'in front of the leg' and, in fact, behind the bit with the neck lowered. This is purely a means to an end and not a method that should be abused; neither should it be used by inexperienced riders unless under the guidance of an experienced instructor.

There has been much controversy about the use of 'deep and round' and I believe this is owing to inadequately trained riders having no understanding of the technique, or perhaps some strong riders who abuse it as a means of protracted domination. It, like so many training methods and techniques, can be misused.

There are, however, occasions when such methods are appropriate and can be of great use particularly with a horse who has been badly trained previously, for example, in which case the methods must be applied by an experienced trainer. The method may be used once or even repeated over a short period, but we should always work towards lightness (my maxim is, 'as much strength as is necessary but as light as possible') and release and reward. However, I should emphasize that lightness is not achieved as a result of the horse dropping behind the bit and thus relinquishing contact.

With deep and round, the horse's neck is stretched out at the level of the withers and rounded to the point where the nose comes behind the vertical. To bring a horse's head into this position, a stronger hand may need to be used initially, but the horse must not be allowed to come behind the leg. This gives the rider control over a horse who is inclined to rush off with his nose in the air, or some similar unruliness. By riding into the hand and getting the horse's nose down, or even behind the bit for a while, control can be achieved first. Then the hand can lighten and merely converse with the mouth until the horse has changed his pattern of work and is strong enough to carry his own head whilst moving in good rhythm. The horse can then follow the hand to the best position for his stage of training.

I must reiterate that this method, like many, has a place *at some stage with some horses*, but it is not to be confused with the strong-hand technique seen in many dressage warm-up arenas, where even some of the most advanced

Working the horse deep and round. Colette Sossaman competing in Dallas on her pure-bred stallion Jovial.

horses are driven continuously behind the bit to the point where the nose is touching the chest, and the head is also pulled around to the rider's boot on both sides. At Grand Prix level one would hope that a horse is 'well dressed' and this should not be necessary.

There are, however, some horses who can produce excellent work but remain difficult all their lives. There was a well-known Lusitano stallion who had to be lunged for two hours before anyone could ride him, even when he was twenty-two years old. This example just proves that we should not be too quick to judge a trainer's, or rider's, methods until we know the reasons that lie behind them. It is the constant unnecessary abuse that I abhor.

LONG AND LOW

With this technique, the horse has his neck lowered with the poll well below the withers and his nose out in front of the vertical, which persuades the horse to lengthen his neck and open out the throat area.

Long and low is an excellent way to work the willing and quiet horse into a relaxed and rhythmical walk and trot. Once the head is down you are able to encourage more forward movement that is, in fact, improving the stride. By holding the reins softly and giving them at every opportunity the horse is in no way restricted or held back and less leg is necessary, thus a good habit of less leg and hands becomes a precedent. Here we are looking for good regularity of movement and balance; just letting the reins go is not good practice with dangerously excitable horses.

Iberian horses, particularly the stallions, can have big, heavy necks, giving them a lot of weight to carry and balance. They can also be deeper at the point from below the ears to the throat than many other riding horses. This can make working with the nose vertical very difficult and so it must be nursed into this position over a long period. The temptation to force the head carriage with continuously strong hands will result in tension and a lack of impulsion, and will require even stronger legs to back the hands up. This preoccupation with an 'advanced' head carriage is common amongst riders and trainers and encourages harsh and strong treatment which only increases in severity as time goes on if the problem is not remedied.

Whenever there is an issue I feel needs to be remedied, I like to proceed on the principle of what I call 'working in opposites', that is, whatever the horse tends to do naturally I will work towards the opposite effect.

Horses with big necks who are tight in the throat tend to carry their heads high with a hollow back; with their noses stuck out they can prove difficult to work, as they find it very hard to bring their faces onto the vertical plane. These horses also often come with the added problem of comparatively weak quarters. If schooled badly from the start they will tend to use their necks and front legs to pull themselves forward rather than push from the 'engine' in the rear. It is wise to give these horses freedom of movement in the walk and trot to strengthen the quarters first by teaching them to lower the neck to develop the back and gain impulsion, and then slowly bring the nose to the vertical as their education advances. There is no quick fix for this problem. With some of these horses it may in fact be appropriate to be able to bring the horse behind the vertical and ask for extra stretch in the deep and round position, in order to encourage them to round their backs. This, however, needs to be done with great tact if it is not to prove counter-productive. The nose should not be maintained in this position but you should be able to place the nose behind the vertical at will as an exercise. This is a position that will give you more control as you need it but you should not rely on, and always work in, this outline.

As work becomes consistent and the hindquarters become strong, the attempt should be made to bring the head carriage up progressively whilst always maintaining the habit of relaxing the neck down before and after work, but never allowing the horse to just potter along. You are also able to revert to this lowered position for both relaxation and reward at any time during training when something strenuous has been performed or a new goal has been achieved, however small. Because the large necks are so heavy, the musculature of the top line and back must become strong to carry the front end correctly and without support from the rider, that is, the horse must be in self-carriage.

To achieve the lowering of the neck and seeking of the bit may not be as easy as it sounds. Merely letting the horse have a free rein does not necessarily get the head down as you would wish as, often, the tendency is for the horse to revert to working hollow with the nose pointing forward.

A good method for lowering the neck, in my opinion, is to walk on a 20 m circle with the outside rein absolutely still at about withers level; give a light nudge with the inside leg, followed quickly but calmly with a softly applied closing of the inside hand at the same height, then relax the fingers and give first the inside hand followed immediately by the outside hand. Follow the movement of the neck and mouth, giving only with the movement in harmony with the stride. If possible, give the rein more in each stride if your horse's head and neck continue to stay down and he continues to move forward. At the moment you give with both hands the horse may have a tendency to slow down; you should then send him forward with the inside leg again. Initially, you will have to repeat this many times until the horse understands and lowers his head at the first indication. Remember to give with the movement *only if the horse follows the hand down to the correct position*. It is futile to give if the nose goes up.

With this exercise, the aim is to get the poll below the height of the withers, or even further down, without the horse pulling at you harshly. If he should pull, then urge him forwards onto the bit and try again. The aim is to be able to go progressively further and further down, and so each time your horse lifts his head you must repeat the exercise. Remember, once the horse has lowered his head and neck so far and you want to go down lower, the action of the hands should be subtle enough to act on the mouth where it is and not to bring the head back up to the starting point again. The exercise should be progressive and should improve over time and, as the horse becomes stronger and more familiar with the exercise, it will become easier.

The Walk

The walk is said to be the mother of all gaits and this is so true, but it is a gait that so many ignore, preferring to trot a horse to near exhaustion before a walk can even be achieved.

I spend a lot of time in walk both in and out of the school and insist that all my horses, regardless of the discipline for which they are destined, walk purposefully forward, are able to walk both briskly and slowly at my request and, most importantly, walk without having to be constantly nagged by the leg. I achieve this right from the start by allowing the horses the freedom to walk, first on the lunge and then under saddle, beginning each lesson with walk for as long a period as I feel necessary. This not only enables you to calm and relax the horse without the need to exhaust him, but it also means you can supple the horse with progressively decreasing circles and lateral work, as and when he learns it, without the risk of damage to unprepared muscles. Ending the lesson with a period of walk is also important for relaxing the horse after a good work-out.

Starting work at walk may seem an obvious thing to do, but there are many horses who cannot contain their enthusiasm and trot or canter around before any sense can be attained. This can quickly become a habit if the trainer allows it to go on; a habit that can be exacerbated by the horse having to stay in the box for several days, for whatever reason. The routine of walking first is, therefore, particularly helpful when bringing a horse back into work after rest or injury.

As early as possible in a horse's training I prepare a series of walk exercises for him that give him a routine with which he can prepare mentally and physically for the task of learning something new or confirming or improving what is already within his repertoire. Once the routine is familiar to the horse, he will immediately be at ease, knowing that the work is within his capabilities. Every horse is different, as indeed are riders, but a simple programme prepares both horse and rider for the work to come.

I begin work on a long rein whenever possible, encouraging long and low work from the beginning, working equally in both directions around the school, starting with 20 m circles and systematically reducing the circles to 6 m in the corners, making sure to change direction frequently. As the horse becomes more adept and is able to do lateral work I add this to his routine, progressing through each new movement in the stages that suit the individual horse. With leg-yielding, for example, I will leg-yield from the centre line to the outer wall, and then progress to leg-yields with increasingly more lateral and less forward movement. Shoulder-in will be executed initially from a 6 m circle down the long side and then on a small circle, from which we will move on to travers and eventually a few half-passes.

The important thing to remember is that this period of working in is for both you and your horse to establish a calm, relaxed and supple way of going in preparation for the work to come. You may need to vary the programme from time to time but I hope you can see that by having this familiar routine you have a 'comfort blanket' to fall back on at times of stress such as a competition or when in unfamiliar surroundings at clinics and shows. It also gives you a good springboard into more complicated work.

Harmonizing Leg and Hand

Asking with the leg at the moment the horse's corresponding hind leg steps through is not widely understood, although it should be a fundamental part of a rider's basic education. The ability to harmonize the legs and hands seems to elude even some of the more 'advanced' riders, many of whom could not ride a finely trained horse because they only know to kick or grip so tightly in a manner that would torment a sensitive horse. We hear so much about light hands but seldom do we hear anything about light legs. Nuno Oliveira spoke many times about tact and finesse and he emphasized that the legs are also to be light and that they have many more actions than that of just kicking.

One of the most important elements of riding in harmony is timing: the moment when to ask. The moment of asking with the leg is so important and yet people are so seldom taught when or even how to do this.

I ask my students to take their feet out of the stirrups and to let their legs hang long and relaxed, and then to hold the reins on the buckle and allow the horse to move actively forward. At this point I ask them to close their eyes and feel their legs 'swing in' alternately: the left leg swings in as the near hind steps forward, and the right leg swings in as the off hind steps forward. In the moment a particular hind leg moves forward, the rider must ask with the leg on the same side, but if the aid is given too soon or too late, the horse will either rush his stride or movement, or ignore the aid altogether.

I so often see hard and inappropriate use of the legs, such as incessant kicking at every stride in an attempt to produce impulsion, or a sort of wiggling of the leg asking the horse to move forward or sideways, which is senseless and achieves very little.

The legs should be still and close, relaxed enough to caress the body of the horse as they give the aids, and not clamped on the horse's sides in a rib-crushing grip in a desperate attempt to compensate for the rider's loss of balance.

Wherever possible it should be the lower inner calf that gives a leg aid. However, for short-legged riders on horses with deep girths it is more difficult to apply the leg without the spur than it is for a long-legged person riding a narrow horse with a small girth. The latter instance gives rise to the opposite problem when the heel is so far below the girth that the rider must bend the leg too much to use the spur. The Spanish Riding School's Lipizzaners are not big horses, and the Austrian riders are often tall so, as their long legs drop well below the girth, they use swan-necked spurs in order to make contact with the horses' sides.

A spur should not be used indiscriminately but only as and when it is required, and the placement of the spur dictates how subtly it can be used. For some, the best position for a spur is at the heel of the boot and not, as so many people wear them, at the ankle. The spurs of the Spanish *vaquera* rider are worn at the heel as are those of the riders in the Royal School in Jerez. This positioning gives the rider the capacity to use the spurs in a number of ways: a stroking action or a squeezing action can be applied, with pressures ranging from the merest brush to quite firm; and for an instant response in an emergency, such as a *vaquera* rider or a *rejoneador* may confront in the country or the bullring, a stronger action can be used.

During training, the ability to vary the rhythm in all gaits is essential. Not only does it develop the horse's gaits through the many nuances from say, a little trot (to use Oliveira's terminology) to a fully extended trot, but it also gives the trainer a greater understanding of what the horse does and how the horse feels when he moves. Co-ordinating the combination of forward propulsion and upward lift can, therefore, come within your grasp as you work towards piaffe, passage, pirouettes and other advanced work.

The use of the rider's legs is an essential part of rhythm and should be practised constantly. For example, if the horse is moving at what seems to be his natural trot and we wish to improve it by making it bigger, we apply the leg at the correct moment to ask him to step further underneath his body and make more effort with each stride. Since we do not wish to move faster with the same length of stride we maintain our own rising-trot rhythm, capture the forward energy produced by the leg aid and hold it for an instant with the hand – an action which should be subtle. By repeating the exercise the horse soon comes to understand that 'bigger' not 'more rapid' is required. This understanding should be developed in all gaits.

If we actually wish to make the horse move faster by taking more rapid

Light contact, a settled mouth and a steady but 'forward' trot – a rider from the Yeguada Susaeta on Decreto.

strides we can repeat the asking with the leg at a rhythm slightly faster than that at which he is actually working, and rise out of the seat faster and with more effort. As soon as he understands what is required, he will speed up his stride pattern to accommodate you. You should need only to convey the rhythm you want and it is to be hoped that the horse will maintain it without having to be constantly reminded. You must 'ask and allow', judging exactly how much you do need to remind him to maintain the required length of stride and rhythm.

By putting your horse on a 20 m circle you can set off at a certain speed in rising trot and practise getting him more forward-going by putting more effort into the pelvis coming through towards the hands. You can then slow things down again by making less effort. Ask for the same thing each time in the same position on the circle – when crossing the centre line for example – and then you will find that on each circle you can use less hand and leg until the horse just follows the rhythm of your body. After a while, the horse will associate the place with the request and will anticipate the change; you can thus, once more, seek to 'whisper' your command rather than 'shout'. You will then have to confirm the training in other places in the arena so that he learns to associate the aids, rather than the place, with the request.

Young horses will find it particularly difficult to work through corners and on circles without obeying their natural instinct to slow down and take smaller steps. This is also a rider's natural instinct. To avoid this it is necessary to encourage the horse to keep to the same rhythm through the corners, but do not ask for a tighter corner than he is capable of doing at any stage. You can make more demands on his balance and agility by going deeper into the corners as his confidence and schooling improve.

To prevent this urge to slow down in the corners it is also good to vary the rhythm in different places around the arena, in particular on the straight sides before the corners; slowing down prior to the corners and then asking for a little more speed going through the corners will stop the horses thinking 'corners always mean slowing down'.

Lateral Work and Preparation for the More Advanced Movements

Starting Lateral Work

Once all three basic gaits are suitably well developed the next step is to approach the turns on the forehand and haunches, and lateral work in the forms of shoulder-in, half-pass, travers and renvers. As the aim of this book is to discuss the general process of training and not the specifics and technicalities of the movements per se, I will not elaborate on every movement, aid and training process, but will talk more about the reasoning behind, and attitudes to, the movements. Many fine trainers have detailed the development of these lateral movements, and I recommend you study as many as you can.

The lateral work should be approached systematically and progressively – following through logically from one movement to another. This process continues throughout training; for example, the lateral work discussed in this section, in tandem with the development of the canter, will lay the foundations for the canter pirouettes.

Some trainers like to introduce lateral work from the beginning in a 'big' trot, perhaps because of a concern that there is insufficient energy developed at the walk. Personally, I prefer to start lateral work in the walk. This I believe gives horse and rider – particularly when they are not so experienced – the time to understand and feel the movement. The key is to make just a few good steps at first and gradually increase the number. (In addition to its role in helping the horse to understand what is required, I feel the lateral work at walk has a grace and beauty when it is performed calmly and correctly.)

At the beginning, then, in each gait, I work in a rhythm that the horse finds comfortable, which should be encouraging in the early stages, giving him confidence and a relaxed way of going. Once the movement itself is understood, improvement can be worked on, asking the horse to move 'bigger' in each stride. It seems that the trend with some trainers, in particular trainers of the big Warmbloods, is to insist on a medium trot from the moment the horse enters the arena, always looking for the bigger movement; I prefer to allow the horse to grow into the bigger trot. Not all horses are capable of a big trot and it can be difficult for them; they tend to fall out of it when not in straight lines and in particular in the lateral work.

I believe that all horses should be given every opportunity to develop their full potential, but we cannot demand of them that which is not within their capacity to give. The horse will naturally slow down or grind to a halt if he finds the work difficult; more leg will, therefore, be required – but not before you understand what the difficulty is. There is little point in making the exercise too demanding and then merely expecting the horse to do it by kicking harder. It is rather like shouting 'Two lagers, *por favor*'; if a Spanish waiter does not speak English, he does not speak English – however loudly you shout.

Peter Maddison-Greenwell and Farolero in half-pass left at passage.

In the half-pass, for example, we vary the extent of the forward movement in proportion to the sideways movement in progressive exercises. The more forward and less sideways movement being the easier option; shortening the forward movement and increasing the sideways movement makes it more difficult.

By varying the rhythm as you flow along the wall or across the arena you create the ability to improve by making just a few demanding strides at a time then settling to a movement you are both comfortable with. This builds confidence and develops the power to pick up and continue when a movement has lost impulsion.

THE CANTER AND FLYING CHANGES

The same principle of developing confidence and power is true of the canter. To be able to canter big and bold across the diagonal, or to canter on the spot in preparation for the pirouette is the aim of any trainer wishing to go to Grand Prix or *Alter Esquela* level, whether it be for competition or pleasure. Spanish and Lusitano horses do, by and large, have an innate ability to lower the haunches and still remain in canter, giving them the capacity for good pirouettes, for which they often make good scores in competition.

It must be understood, however, that this does not mean *every* Spanish and Lusitano horse can achieve this. I have said to people time and time again that, whilst they are wonderful horses, they do not automatically 'come out of the toy box' doing these advanced movements. Many horses can be trained to do what may look like advanced movements to the uninitiated but they are not necessarily good dressage horses. Few and far between are horses of *any* breed that have the three good gaits, the right conformation, the talent and the trainability to go to the top; if it were but that easy!

There is a lot of work to be done on the canter to prepare the horse before the change of leg or the pirouette should be considered. Some say that the Spanish horse finds flying changes difficult, but I have had no trouble teaching many Spanish horses to change at the canter (*galope*); it's stopping them from changing that can become the problem! In all seriousness, it is not a difficult task to teach a flying change, it is the getting it as and when you want it that is more difficult – and this reliability is what you need to give you the opportunity to develop multiple (or 'tempi') changes.

Again, it is the power coming through from behind that makes a good change. The tendency for many horses, and certainly any horse who is not strong behind, is to be late. Changing the front end is relatively simple but if the back end does not change at the same time it is neither comfortable nor correct, as the horse then becomes disunited, i.e. it is as if the two ends of the horse would canter in different directions if they were not attached in the middle.

The right time to ask for the first change of leg is debatable. In dressage it is usual to establish lateral work before working on the changes of leg. Some riders in low-level showjumping competitions or out hunting often leave the horse to his own devices. In the show ring a horse must execute a single change if he is to impress the judges, and at higher levels of showjumping, or in sports such as polo, the horse must learn the change to be able to turn quickly and be well balanced for the next jump or next change of direction. However, these changes are not the same as the fluent, precise, yet expressive flying change performed at the rider's will, which is essential if the horse and rider are to cope with the very demanding three-time, two-time and one-time (tempi) changes.

Teaching changes after lateral work is logical when you take into consideration the fact that the majority of competition horses are big, strong Warmbloods who find it easier to be straight than some Iberian horses, who are very supple and agile and tend to have very mobile quarters. Care must be taken, therefore, to ensure that Iberians move straight. They do, however, find lateral work easy, and so it is often the case that at the time you approach your flying changes, a Spanish horse will deviate from straightness if he is oversensitive to the outside leg aid. This must, of course, always be addressed as the next change will become almost impossible if the horse is crooked. With a Spanish horse, therefore, it might be a consideration that teaching the change could be started before the lateral work has gone too far down the line. In this way the horse will not be too sensitive to the outside leg and keep bringing the quarters in each time you use the outside leg, thus giving you a travers-like movement instead of a correct (straight) canter. The other point to consider is that, if the horse is highly sensitive to the outside leg, the onus is on the rider to apply it with great discretion.

There are many ways to approach the first single flying change, and the wise trainer prepares carefully with many strikes-off in both directions until the horse becomes foot perfect. The horse should also be well balanced in counter-canter (an exercise that has value in improving suppleness and straightness) and be able to continue around the arena in this gait without falling into trot. One reason why the counter-canter is so important as a preparation for the flying changes is that you do not wish your horse to think that every time he goes to the left he must be on the left leg and vice versa, otherwise when to change becomes the horse's decision. It is for good reason that counter-canter is a part of dressage tests as well as the *doma vaquera* competition.

Going from canter to trot to canter, gradually reducing the trot to a single stride, is a simple way many choose to start flying-change work. Using the long side to prepare for, and the first corner of the short side to ask for, the change is prudent. Being in counter-canter on the long side as you approach the corner (which would normally, in canter, represent a quarter of a 10 m circle) gives you the opportunity to ask for the change where the horse him-self would naturally want to be on the inside leg.

Should this be successful on the first attempt, return to walk and make much of the horse. Trying the change again in the same place might be a good idea, but do not overdo it; be happy with a good change because this is a mile-stone in any horse's education and I believe it alters the whole way in which you can train from now on. There is little more frustrating than to have to return to trot to change direction; certainly for any choreographed display work it is the one component that holds you back from performing a fluent and pleasing show.

Two other methods of introducing the flying change are half-passing to the wall and changing at the wall, using the wall and the corner to help, and riding across a diagonal and changing as you approach the new direction.

There are, in fact, many approaches that can be adopted to achieve the flying change and many trainers have their own particular favourite. I believe it is important to learn and experience as many methods as possible because, as with all training, there is never just one way of achieving a result. So often, knowing another method can make the difference between a particular movement being learned or not.

Whichever method you use, be prepared for your horse to start to antici-pate the change. The Iberian horse is intelligent and often anticipates in order to please. This most certainly does not warrant punishment but a change of approach perhaps, and certainly establishing a good canter before you try the change again.

Once the single change in both directions is consolidated, it is then time to perfect it by developing balance in the change as well as having the power to perform an expressive one. A good way to obtain this is to work in a bigger canter, changing on the long side with a bold and co-ordinated stride, which gives volume to the movement. An exercise to help you attain this is as fol-lows. Begin counter-canter from walk at the approach to the short side, keep-ing steady around the corner until you straighten, increase the volume of the canter for a few strides, make your change, return to walk, halt, rein-back, strike off in counter-canter and begin the exercise again. In order to keep both your and your horse's composure, you need time and space to perform this exercise and this is easier when you have a 60 x 20 m arena.

If you do not have a full-size arena, use the great outdoors. A horse will often not only benefit from the change of scenery but will also give you more energy and spring, which is going to make the change more expressive. Adversely, some horses might give too much energy to, and get over-excited by, the flying change in the open, giving them the excuse to 'run through your hands' immediately after the change. This is quite typical for some horses in the early stages but must not be allowed to get out of hand.

The one-time changes (changes of leg at every stride) constitute an extremely demanding exercise for any horse and rider, which commands a high degree of concentration, rhythm and balance. To progress from single changes to multiple changes must, again, be a gradual process over a long period, but if you can do one change you can do two, so long as the distance between each change gives you enough time to collect your thoughts and align yourself and your horse ready for the next one. This can only be achieved with lots of practice and only when you and your horse are ready. If the work is rushed, your horse will start to change without you. Even when you think you have everything right and have done a good job, once you get to multiple changes, some Spanish horses are so agile and clever that they can change in the blink of an eye and, whilst you think you are cantering quietly to the left, with just a minor twitch of the underwear you will have done two changes. When this occurs all you can do is return to establishing a good canter and single changes until you believe your horse is calm enough to attempt multiples again. This may take days, and sometimes it is as well to leave changes for a while, but when you come back to them later you will be surprised by how much he has remembered.

There are, of course, many more movements and methods that could be discussed, the criteria for which would demand a book in its own right. In this section I have, therefore, concentrated only on those movements with which I have found riders of Spanish horses to have specific problems, either because they lack experience and/or because they over- or underestimate the abilities of the Spanish horse.

Observations on Multi-disciplinary Riding

Before defining the training for *doma vaquera*, *doma clasica* or competition dressage, I would like to emphasize the difficulties that can arise from mixing these disciplines. Up to a certain point the training procedure is much the same for all three disciplines, or, for that matter, for any ridden horse; that is, from the groundwork through backing, on to basic circles and straight lines, plus the 'campaign' work in the country and on the roads.

But there is a stage at which the paths divide. Those who wish to train for *vaquera* work should go down the *serreta* route (see page 169), but the *vaquera* training should not be followed any further if you wish to ride in a *doma clasica* class or an FEI dressage competition at a later stage; going back to a snaffle or double bridle and the more classical movements after *vaquera* training might be more difficult than you think.

The Spanish *vaquera* riders and trainers who have been doing this all their lives know what they are doing, whether they are producing horses for work or competition. However, while the general training is the same, the quality of the working horse's movement is not judged so long as it is effective and the work gets done whereas, in competition, the better the quality of the performance, the more successful horse and rider will be.

People with much less experience, particularly those outside Spain, who might wish to ride *vaquera* for pleasure but also use the same horse for show classes, classical work or competition dressage, *must* realize how difficult that can be. Some horses can cope with it, but it is a lot to ask of any horse to do one, let alone all, of the disciplines well. I will explain more about the differences and consequent problems later in this chapter.

For those who do wish to do multi-disciplinary riding, I would advise you to consolidate the classical training first and only introduce the *vaquera* bridle and saddle gradually once the horse is truly forward, working from the leg, halting without resistance, performing most of his work at canter (including the lateral work) on the bit, has started the canter changes and, most importantly, can bend throughout his body around your inside leg into the outside rein, maintaining an inside flexion without the constant use of your inside hand. At this stage it is to be hoped that it will not take too much revision for him, after the *vaquera* training, to return without confusion from curb-only bitting to a double bridle, and to a totally different type of saddle. I certainly have a number of horses who are capable of doing *vaquera* and *clasica*, but I always remind myself not to expect perfection in any one area if I am continually changing the goalposts.

It is possible to introduce the *vaquera* tack earlier than the stage suggested if you wish only to do showing classes. Showing and parade classes demand little more of the horse and rider than to look the part and to do a few circles and straight lines in company. Without belittling this, if this is as far as you wish to go, then the schooling need not be as thorough as for work or serious competition. However, in Spain *doma vaquera* is the most popular of all equestrian activities and so the demands and expectations are much higher – in which case the more thorough you are, the further you will go.

Doma Vaquera

I intend to cover the *doma vaquera* training in some detail because this will be far less familiar to people who may already be fairly au fait with classical training.

The *doma vaquera* movements remain deeply rooted in the old traditions of ranch work in the same way that many of the *doma clasica* movements originate from the training of horses for war. In this section I would like to give an introduction to this fascinating work by explaining some of the *vaquera* training methods and the execution of the *vaquera* movements, and compare them to those of *doma clasica* and competition dressage.

Everything the working horse does in the country will be mirrored in the *vaquera* competition arena. As in the classical and competition schools, *vaquera* riders should be looking for good rhythm and a correct way of going, both for their own and their horses' comfort and well-being; such aims will, in fact, prolong the working life of a horse who spends much of his time per-forming strenuous, and sometimes dangerous, manoeuvres. *Doma vaquera* is tough and demanding, the horses are the equestrian equivalent of rugby play-ers; it is a case of no nonsense, get the job done, and don't mind the knocks. Having said that, I see an ever-increasing number of good *vaquera* riders paying more attention to the welfare of their horses, and they are more will-ing to learn good techniques and methods of training.

Vaquera work is ancient, as are some of the methods and equipment used, the *serreta* for example. Other elements of *vaquera* equipment that are unique to Spain are the traditional saddle and bridle. This equipment (see Chapter 7) is still used in the fields today and must be used in all *doma vaquera* competition.

The *Serreta*

The *serreta* is now used only by the Spanish and the Portuguese and perhaps those enthusiasts outside Spain who wish to use the techniques, equipment and methods of the *vaquera* rider. Probably the nearest piece of equestrian equipment to the *serreta* in other parts of the world is the bosal (*bozal*), which is used in varying forms in the Americas. The bosal is usually a braided leather or rawhide noseband that works on the same part of the nose as the *serreta*. Some taper into a heel knot that works on the sensitive nerves of the chin; and the Peruvian bosal, for example, is fitted by being tied at the back of the muzzle. Bosals can be used to bend and flex the horse's neck in the same way that a *serreta* does. In Chapter 7 I explained what the *serreta* looks like and how it should fit; now I will describe what it is used for.

The training of the *vaquera* horse begins with the *serreta*, which for training purposes is used with just a sliphead and a throatlash, like a cavesson. It works by applying pressure to the nose in the same position as that of a drop noseband. Here, the bone is hard but nevertheless sensitive and the *serreta* should be handled with consideration. This piece of equipment may appear severe to some, and it certainly can be in the wrong hands, but when used correctly it is an extremely useful tool.

The horse's first introduction to the *serreta* will be when he is led and presented in-hand, and then he will progress to being lunged from it. Once the horse understands circles, and stops and starts on cue, he will progress to work with a saddle and side reins. His training will then progress with the acceptance of a bit and a rider. The *serreta* certainly has an essential role to play in the training of horses for stock work, the bullring and the *doma vaquera* competition arena.

STALLIONS

The *serreta* will keep a lively young stallion under control when a headcollar or even a lungeing cavesson will not. Remember, nearly all male horses in Spain are kept entire and, even taking into account the good natures these horses have, sex is sex and control must be exercised until the horses understand that they must not allow themselves to be distracted when working. I have seen some strong men in England struggle with, and lose, a stallion who was wearing just a cavesson.

At the Spanish breed shows in Britain it is a rule that all stallions presented without a rider or being worked or handled in public must wear *serretas*, which must have a throatlash, or bridles. This is a very sensible precaution to reduce the chances of stallions being out of control amongst other stallions, mares and indeed the general public.

The *serreta* is generally used to present the stallion for showing classes, although in Spain other devices are now being used, such as leather half nose-bands with a chain that closes tighter around the nose when the lead rein is pulled, in the same way a choke chain does on a dog.

My view is that early introduction of the *serreta* to a stallion is very beneficial as he needs to accept it for presentation and handling, which may happen before he is broken. Having handled many Spanish and Lusitano stallions and colts over the years, I have found that they almost all instinct-ively take to the *serreta* right from the very beginning.

LUNGEING AND SIDE REINS

When the horse has been handled and socialized, he moves on to getting used to the bit, bridle, saddle and side reins whilst on the lunge. Initially we want to teach the horse to move on a circle, for which a one-ring *serreta* with a throatlash can be used; no other tack is needed. Once circling, halting, and changing rhythm and gait to your command, he can be introduced to the bridle with a snaffle; at this stage the *serreta* needs only to be on a sliphead, which should be run through the browband and under the headpiece. The horse can get used to the snaffle resting in his mouth while he still responds to the *serreta*. When lungeing, it is the *serreta* that encourages the horse to look to the inside.

The next stage is to add the roller and side reins. Because of the easy-going nature of many Spanish horses, some people bypass the roller and put a saddle on right from the start, but you must know the horse well and have the experience to make the correct judgement about this. If a saddle is used it should be an English or continental saddle (perhaps one which is deep and has rolls in front and behind the knee and thigh for the rider's first few sessions); the *vaquera* saddle should not be used at this stage. I always use an old saddle with a well-padded numnah for breaking a horse in as accidents do happen occasionally and it is foolish to risk one's favourite, expensive competition saddle.

When the roller, or saddle, is first put on it is advisable to have some expe-rienced help; do not put this equipment on in the stable, just in case the horse bucks or kicks against the unfamiliar sensation. The roller or girth should be tightened gently and gradually to help avoid any untoward reaction from the horse. However, the horse will usually settle quickly and as he becomes accus-tomed to the roller or saddle you can then add the side reins. These must always be buckled initially at a length that does not restrict the horse's head and neck too much in case he objects, and only shortened gradually to the desired length. The routine for each day is to lunge without side reins first and then, when they are attached, to shorten them a step at a time, but never to force the horse into a position behind the bit.

The side reins can be attached to the snaffle rings or, as this is training for the *vaquera* horse, you may choose to attach them to a three-ringed *serreta*, but leave the snaffle in the mouth with no reins attached to it. Thus the horse becomes accustomed to the primary action being on the nose, not on the mouth. Long-reining is the next stage and the long-reins will also be attached to the *serreta*.

Once you feel that the time is right to mount, make sure, again, that you have some experienced assistance and take the whole procedure as slowly and calmly as possible. If all goes well the horse will have little objection to you being up on top and within a matter of days schooling can begin in earnest.

Now you will advance to two sets of reins: one pair, traditionally split (not buckled or sewn together), to the *serreta* rings and one pair to the snaffle. I advise that you put loose-fitting side reins on the bit for some time before you actually start to ride, then the horse will not be surprised by the feeling of the bit being used by the rider when first it happens.

The principle of this system of working from the nose is to avoid the use of the mouth too much, making it more sensitive and lighter for the future when the curb is brought in.

You may use the three-ringed *serreta* to flex and bend the horse and only use the snaffle rein sparingly or as you see fit. You must follow all the basic principles of bending and flexing without twisting the head and always try to use a light hand.

UP TO THE BRIDLE

A mature, schooled *vaquera* horse will be ridden in a bridle with a single rein on a curb bit. The *serreta* is left on the noseband as a reminder to the horse but is not attached to a rein. In this situation, the *serreta* has two leather keepers through which the noseband slides. Younger horses may have either a second rein on the bit, thus making the action of the curb more like a Pelham, or have the second rein on the *serreta*. The traditional noseband can accommodate a *serreta* with two rings which are screwed into place on the noseband, thus the *serreta* throatlash and sliphead are not needed. The *serreta* can still be used to bend and flex the horse and keep the horse 'in your hand' from the nose rather than the mouth.

The effect of a curb bit is definitely enhanced by the *serreta* but the effect and technique of using both items must be well understood before embarking on their use, particularly together; if they are mishandled they can be severe.

The system should have a natural progression from handling and lungeing to riding – first with the snaffle and *serreta* and then with the curb and *serreta* – so that the maturing horse fully understands both the *serreta* and the curb. The practical reason behind the curb is the element of control with a single rein. An experienced rider with good hands can achieve not only a refinement of movement but also a great deal of control, which is necessary during advanced movements. A sudden halt from the gallop, or keeping your horse in the ultimate collection through a demi-pirouette, ready to surge forward into gallop again, would not be easy for anyone using a snaffle in one hand.

THE WRONG SIDE OF THE *SERRETA*

When horses appear to have been badly treated with the *serreta*, with white hair or scarring on their noses, it is the user not the *serreta* that is to blame. The *serreta* must be maintained with a good covering of leather otherwise it will rub the nose to the point where a sore, or a deeper flesh wound, can be opened up. There are good and bad trainers and practices in every field and every country, and we must consider that some horses, through no fault of their own, have been made dangerous by ignorance and bad handling. It must also be remembered that people are often dealing with stallions, some of whom may be strong-willed; in the wrong hands, horses of this ilk can become dangerous.

It is a brave man who will take a horse like this on and take control, sometimes having to use measures that would not ordinarily be approved of to get the job done. In the end, if the horse becomes well-mannered, obedient and can lead a productive (and, it is to be hoped, happy) life, the ends can sometimes justify the means.

I make no apology for re-emphasizing the fact that horses can be made dangerous by ignorance and bad handling, for which there is no excuse.

The *Vaquera* Walk

As stated earlier, the basis of all good work is the walk. The *vaquera* walk is a purposeful gait as there is a place to go and work to be done, and it can be sustained for long periods. When training, it is good to spend a great deal of time developing this walk in the country, negotiating every natural obstacle: through and over ditches, over logs and through gates, and going up and down hills, in order to gain confidence, fitness and strength. No slouching along is allowed for a working horse, he is not out for a stroll in the park; the gait must come 'through' from behind and have a fluent and rhythmical, swinging stride.

In walk, both for the competition arena and for work, the horse must be able to turn on the forehand both into the bend and away from the bend in one continuous flow; perform quarter, half and full turns, or *vueltas*, (turns on the haunches), half-passes, zigzag half-passes (and, at an advanced level, full passes) and collect and extend the walk. The horse must also be able to rein-back half the length of an arena quickly.

The *Media Vuelta*

A movement possibly unique to the stock horse is the turn of 180 degrees in one stride, developed from the turn on the haunches. For the *vaquera* horse this is the *media vuelta* (half turn); the equivalent move for the Western horse is the roll-back. From the walk the horse appears to perform a small levade, sinking his haunches, lifting his front legs, and pivoting on his hind legs to turn to face the direction from which he came. This, when done well, is a graceful movement and shows great control. It is also performed at the canter and can be practised at the trot, but will not be performed at the trot in the competition arena.

Once you have established a turn on the haunches at a fluent walk, the *media vuelta* should be introduced at the walk, initially turning through just 90 degrees using each of the four corners of a square in turn. The turn on the haunches is most important because, if you have any problems with the *media vuelta*, you must be able to return to the simpler movement to set you up again. When executing the *media vuelta* the horse must remain calm, but the effort required is far greater than that for a turn on the haunches as the horse must physically carry more weight on the hind end as both front legs leave the ground; in fact, the greater part of the weight of both horse and rider is carried momentarily by the quarters.

The aids for the 90 degree *vuelta* are the same as those for a quarter turn on the haunches, but are, in fact, applied almost all at once and with more effort as you intend to make the 90 degree turn in one stride and not several walking strides. This may take some time for the first-time *vaquera* trainer or rider to master and is better learned with experienced *vaquera* help; this movement has no equivalent in modern-day dressage so few trainers outside Spain will understand it. Once the turn is completed, the horse must be asked to walk forwards immediately because you are looking for flow in the exercise. It is wise to do this on a square of approximately 16 m so as to give you and your horse the time and distance to compose yourselves before the next attempt. If either of you is not composed, continue the square but go back to the quarter turn on the haunches. This way you do not set yourself up to fail but indeed revert to a simpler movement until ready to try again.

Once this has been assimilated, progress to the half turn. The same aids are applied, but by now the principle of the movement is understood and so the aids should be lighter. However, if necessary, apply a stronger aid and turn your shoulders and your abdomen as one unit, taking your hand (you should be working towards riding one-handed by now) to the inside to a greater degree than for the quarter turn at the moment the horse lifts his forelegs. Here, your outside leg becomes especially relevant to control the quarters. The turn can be increased to the full 180 degrees with practice and good timing. By doing this along a wall, say 1 m (3¼ ft) in from the wall, the horse is encouraged to walk straight between each attempt. The wall also helps you to keep control of the quarters, as the temptation is for the horse to swing his quarters out when he finds this difficult. The horse halts momentarily before each turn.

The smart horse may start to anticipate the *media vuelta* each time you halt, turning before you have a chance to prevent it. Consequently, you must neither overdo the exercise nor punish him for the anticipation. It is far better to go back to the walk turns on the haunches, simple halts and rein-backs (see below) before returning to this new movement. When you do revise the movement, make the halt before the turn longer, vary the places in which the exercise is executed and put other exercises in between the half turns, keeping the horse alert but calm.

With a slower or less excitable horse who has less motivation, it is possible to perform the exercise repeatedly if the execution is good; this builds up strength and agility. The horse should not, however, be made tired, or taken to the point of boredom, just because you are getting the hang of it. As with all exercises, stop before the horse wants to stop, leaving him fresh and willing for another day.

Perfecting the *media vuelta* may take years for rider and horse. It is something to be returned to frequently in order to improve the movement as the horse becomes stronger and works more on his haunches, and the rider becomes more proficient.

The Halt

When the *vaquera* horse halts he must be square, on the bit and totally immobile, but engaged, alert and ready to spring into any movement or gait, forwards or backwards.

In my opinion, immobility is the key to so much. Control, submission, expectancy, call it what you will, if you cannot halt and stay in halt you do not have control. Immobility at the halt must be instilled at the very beginning of a horse's training. From the moment you first back the horse, when you mount he must stand until you ask him to move; when he has finished work he must stand to attention until you allow him to stand down; and he must stand solid as a rock until you have dismounted.

Whilst a square halt will take some time to perfect, it is the standing still that is initially of paramount importance. Once this is learnt and the horse becomes more balanced in his work he will, more often than not, stand square naturally. It is at this stage that you consolidate the lesson and concentrate on always getting a square halt, no matter what speed or gait you halt from, until it becomes second nature to the horse. It is also important to ensure that the horse stands for some time before moving off and after halting.

If you omit this good practice from your training regime, or only pursue it intermittently, it is your fault if, at a later stage, the horse does not halt and stand well but becomes a fidget.

The Rein-back

The *vaquera* rein-back is more active and covers a greater distance than the movement in competition dressage, and for good reason; if you have to retreat briskly from a bull it is safer to do it backwards so that you can keep an eye on him, and six to twelve steps may not be enough to put you at a safe distance before you dare turn the horse, and thus your back, on the bull.

Do not, under any circumstances, try to teach the rein-back too early; you must have a forward-going, obedient horse or you will end up with a horse who naps faster backwards than he goes forwards.

Reining-back is not a case of pulling until the horse moves backwards. You must ask the horse to go forward from your leg and then prevent him from doing so by holding the forward movement with your hand (which must not pull), and your seat and back, which is braced momentarily until the horse actually moves backwards. In most cases, asking for only one step back at first and then instantly going forward will help the horse to learn, particularly if he is in the hands of an experienced trainer.

If this is your first attempt, I suggest you pick a particular place in the arena such as the centre of the long side. Ask the horse for a square halt and make sure he stands still; close your legs to ask for the walk forward then close the hand, brace the seat and, once the horse starts to move backwards, tilt your upper body slightly forward, thus lightening the seat and allowing the horse to move without his movement being blocked.

Once the principle is learnt and you are able to do this anywhere in the school you can ask for more steps back. When the horse is moving back, try asking for each further step by applying the legs alternately, in harmony with the horse's hind legs.

Asking the horse to move backwards *for any distance* must come considerably later in his training, after the rein-back has been well established. At this stage of developing the rein-back you can ride rein-back to trot to rein-back and then do the same with the canter. Fully trained *vaquera* horses can rein-back, go forward into gallop, rein-back half the length of the arena, and gallop forwards again to a perfect square halt and total immobility without being over-excited by this movement. During training, these movements will be executed with a halt or half-halt between them, but in competition the horse performs them in one flowing movement.

The Canter and the Trot

The working horse spends a great deal of his day carrying out manoeuvres at the canter, which must be energy-saving and comfortable, both for himself and the rider. To mirror this, the *vaquera* horse does not trot in the competition arena, but I do now see many top riders warming-up in trot with their horses' heads down and bringing their backs up. This may well be a consequence of the fact that some of Spain's best *vaquera* riders now come from a classical background such as the Royal School in Jerez.

Handling the Reins

There is a point at which you change the two pairs of reins (currently, you have one set on the *serreta* rings and one set on the snaffle). The snaffle is now replaced with the black iron *vaquera* curb bit and the *serreta* reins are then placed onto a *serreta*, which, unlike the early-training *serreta*, is attached solely to the traditional noseband, the two rings being screwed to the *serreta* through small holes in the noseband. If this combination of *serreta* and noseband were used with the snaffle, it would restrict the correct loose action of the snaffle because the noseband runs through the bit cheekpieces. As the curb hangs from the bridle cheekpieces its action is only to swivel around the mouthpiece and it does not put pressure on just one corner of the mouth or the other, and so the noseband does not interfere with the bit in any way. Nonetheless, if used heavy-handedly, the curb can have a more severe action than the snaffle because it works on a leverage system – the longer the bit cheekpieces below the mouthpiece, the greater the leverage. When the curb reins are pulled, the mouthpiece rotates and bears down on the tongue with a greater or lesser amount of pressure depending on the size of the port in the mouthpiece and use of the hand.

The curb reins are held on the inside of the *serreta* reins in the same way as they are held in the most common use of a double bridle, i.e. the left snaffle rein is held under the little finger of the left hand and the left curb rein is held under the third finger of the left hand. The right reins are held in the same positions in the right hand.

The other common method of holding the reins whilst training is: the left *serreta* rein is held under the little finger of the left hand, the left curb rein is held under the third finger, the right curb rein under the second finger, and the right *serreta* rein is held in the right hand, which can also carry the switch upright. This is done to prevent the overuse of the curb in bending the horse, as the curb reins are both in one hand. If you wish to bend the horse with the *serreta* rein when circling left, it is simple to rotate the hand at the wrist anti-clockwise (as seen from the rider's view), momentarily putting more pressure on the left *serreta* rein. To bend to the right, the light use of the right hand on the right *serreta* rein can help flex the horse to the right during training, par-ticularly when the horse is having difficulty bending. At all times the inten-tion must be to train the horse to listen to all the leg and body aids, not just the hand, in order to reach the point when the rider can dispense with the *serreta* reins and work the horse with just the curb reins held in the left hand, leaving the right hand free for work. This can only be done by decreasing the use of the hands throughout training. Neither the working nor the competi-tion *vaquera* horse should lean, tug or pull in any way, as the rider must be able to concentrate on the work at hand and not be thinking of the challenge of riding an unruly or heavy-in-the-hand horse; everything must take as little effort as possible.

In the classical school, riders drop the snaffle rein and ride with only the curb to demonstrate that the work is correct and straight and that the snaffle is not needed to flex the head in any of the movements. This originates from the necessity of riding a horse into battle with the reins in the bridle hand,

Vaquera *rider Narciso Arcos warming up. Notice, in the close-up, that both curb reins and one upper rein (in this case, on the single bit) are held in the left hand, with a single upper rein in the right. This, one of several ways of holding the reins, is also used in the Spanish Riding School of Vienna.*

leaving the right hand free for combat. At other times, classical-school riders will use all four reins of the double bridle.

The difference between the work of the classical school or competition dressage and that of the *vaquera* school is immediately evident to any spectator. The immediacy of every action of the *vaquera* horse and rider reminds us that this is a demonstration of work developed amongst the fighting bulls of Spain and not the passive sheep of Wales. The work is strenuous and dangerous and it can be fatal if the horse refuses to move instantaneously where and when asked when working the stock. This principle of instant obedience is carried through to the *vaquera* competition.

In *vaquera* competition, again, use of the second rein must be dispensed with completely; only the curb reins are used and they are always held in the left hand, with the left curb rein under the fourth finger and the right curb rein under the second finger. The ends of the reins are then taken up together and held by the thumb over the first finger, leaving the residue to fall to the right-hand side of the horse's withers. The left hand is held a little above the withers for most of the work, only rising occasionally in the fast halt or rein-back. It is definitely not held as high as that of an American cowboy, but the cowboy does have to keep his hand above the saddle horn, which the *vaquera* saddle does not have.

At the walk, the right hand is placed on the right thigh, and in canter, in front of the sternum, as described on page 25. In competition, the right hand is allowed to shorten the rein and is then returned to its natural position; it is not, however, allowed to flex the horse to the right by pulling on the right rein.

Pirouettes

To the classical and competition dressage rider, the *vaquera* pirouettes would be considered incorrect and, at the very least, too fast. In the classical school, the pirouette is slower, it remains in the three-time beat of the canter and should go through 360 degrees in approximately eight strides; the hindquarters remain virtually on the spot with the hind legs moving in the sequence of the normal canter. For *doma vaquera*, it is the speed combined with the control that needs to be demonstrated. The horse may do as many as two, three or four pirouettes in succession and, as the horse gathers speed, the sequence of the footfall seldom remains in the rhythm of the normal canter. There is also a tendency at times for the horse to pivot around the inside leg when the pirouette is executed on the spot, which is, in itself, not a problem to the working horse nor, therefore, when the competition replicates working practice, as more do it than not. When the movement is seen at its most exciting, a rider will put his horse into a right pirouette, move to the right at maximum speed, then change leg, and go into the left pirouette without so much as leaving the spot.

In this extremely demanding movement the strain is on the inside leg; the more you pivot, the more stress is put on the joints when the ground holds the hoof in place and the front legs take the body mass around this leg. In effect the whole inside leg becomes twisted right up to the stifle joint until it is lifted and replaced on the ground, and this is why the competition dressage riders do not like this movement.

I prefer to teach the horses from the very start not to pivot, but to lift the inside leg. Even at the walk, if the horse is not trained correctly, he will pivot around the planted inside leg and if this is not addressed, it will become a habit that he will carry through to the canter. The reasoning behind my method is to get a good classical canter pirouette wherever possible and then speed it up, rather than just aiming for speed.

As stated, I prefer a classical method of teaching this movement, and there are a number of approaches you can use; here I give two of those methods.

In preparation for the pirouettes, as with the turns on the haunches, you can canter a series of squares in which each corner is considered a quarter pirouette. Keeping the horse in the same three-time canter rhythm on approach to the point of the turn, your back holds the forward movement and, with a half-halt, you canter in effect on the spot. The hands and the upper body turn from the waist to the inside as a single entity; keeping your shoulders and chest in line with the horse's, take the horse's shoulders through 90 degrees in two strides. It is important that the upper body remains upright and the waist does not collapse. As with the shoulder-in, the upper body influences the horse's shoulders, bringing them off, and returning them to, the line. By doing this, you control the degree to which you bring the horse's front end around the hindquarters. If, therefore, the shoulder-in has been understood correctly by both horse and rider, the quarter pirouette should not be too difficult after a little practice.

The rider's legs also have a serious part to play. The outside leg controls the quarters, keeping them in place, and the inside leg asks for impulsion and stops the horse turning further than required, then asks the horse to go forward again, maintaining the canter.

When the quarter pirouettes are correct, you can plan your progress to the half pirouette and eventually the full pirouette. I say 'plan', as you will need to work out exactly where you will try this and from which series of exercises this will work best.

It is the balance of all the aids that are learned in the shoulder-in, travers, renvers and half-passes that prepare for and assist the execution of the pirouette.

Another method is to canter a 20 m circle in travers and reduce the circle until you are able to canter the smallest of travers circles without a loss of rhythm. This is not a movement that is used in *clasica* or competition dressage and so, whilst this method is useful for the introduction of the pirouette and for working on control of the quarters, it will eventually be necessary to be able to ride into the pirouette from a straight line, whether you are training for *vaquera* work, for *clasica* or for competition dressage.

This may seem to be a simple process, and in theory it is, but a pirouette for *vaquera* work, or for the other disciplines, is an advanced movement and should not be considered before both horse and rider are ready, otherwise it becomes a rushed, uncoordinated spin when the rider falls one way and the horse goes the other; a movement with no meaning, use or beauty, instead of the amazing feat of control, balance and agility that it can be.

The Sliding Halt (*Parada a Raya*)

The final movement I will discuss is the sliding halt, which is one of the most dramatic and strenuous movements required of the *vaquera* horse; he is asked to stop from a full gallop, and comes to a halt after a slide of some 3 m (10 ft). There is no loss of impetus at first but the horse goes from the horizontal position of the gallop to a lowering of the quarters as the hocks take a parallel position so far under the body that they are almost touching the ground; the front legs can reach out in front of the nose as much as 45 degrees from the chest. The rider must lean back to keep in balance with the horse and so as not to the load the forehand, which will make this movement more difficult for the horse, but it is not the leaning back that is the aid for the halt; the aid is the bracing of the back supported by the hand in proportion to the sensitivity of the horse. This is one of the most spectacular sights in the *vaquera* arena, which draws great applause from the crowd. The rider repeats this halt several times and is awarded marks for his best one of the day.

As with the transitions of many of the *vaquera* movements, the halt is more sudden than that of the classical and competition schools, and has to be to get the work done. No bull is going to hang around while you have trouble getting your horse to stop or turn precisely at the required moment; he will either decide to cause you real problems or be off over the horizon.

All through the sliding halt training we look for a progressively sharper transition, but must always aim for a good quality halt, only asking the horse for the optimum effort wisely and selectively. In this way the horse's willingness to please you in this movement is neither destroyed by over-exertion in every halt, nor lost completely by doing so few sliding halts that he is not ready when you do need the maximum effort.

By training for sudden downward transitions to halt from each gait, the horse will, if engaged, naturally lower his haunches, even in the walk. Good foundation work in these transitions will ensure that the horse brings his hocks under his body more and more to help him balance as you make more demands of him in the halt.

The difficulty in the canter or gallop to halt transition is that the horse may try to trot first. This is often the result of the horse being too strong in the mouth, often caused by the inexperienced rider or trainer being too heavy-handed with the curb bit, which in turn means that the rider has to put too much effort into achieving the halt. Even just a few strides of trot are not acceptable and so the preparation work for the sliding halts must be thorough and good.

If the head is too low because the horse is leaning on the rider or is otherwise on the forehand then, again, he will not be able to stop as he should. The exercise is only possible if the horse's face is at the vertical, or no more than 5 degrees in front of the vertical, and he is well engaged behind, i.e. he must move in self-carriage.

A good exercise to develop this movement is to work on 20 m circles and follow the sequence of: canter, halt, rein-back and canter. By repeating this sequence you will bring the horse's hind legs further under his body, his centre of balance will move back, making the forehand lighter, and thus the horse will find the halts easier to perform.

Where I believe the *vaquera* trainers stand apart from those of classical and competition dressage horses is the expectation that all *vaquera* horses must be able to do what, to many, will be advanced work, which would not, therefore, usually be considered the domain of every horse. In a relatively short time, a trainer wants to be able to take a young horse out into the country to perform a useful working role. Not only will the youngster be expected to negotiate the difficult obstacles and situations that accompany working with livestock, but he must also demonstrate instant obedience and show no fear when confronted with the intimidating presence of the Spanish fighting bull. The Spanish horse has proved his suitability for the job for many centuries.

The *Garrocha*

Work with the *garrocha* (bull-working pole) starts with the common-sense move of letting the horse see it, smell it and generally get used to seeing it propped up in the school or against the stable before the rider carries it in the saddle. Many horses will trust their riders implicitly but not all are so confident about having such a large item so close to their heads, and can feel threatened.

Make sure that you are confident about taking the step to carrying the *garrocha* in the saddle for the first time; if you are, have someone you trust to assist you by holding the *garrocha*, point upwards, so that you can take it from them, carry it for a few paces – either horizontally or vertically, whichever you judge to be best for you and your horse – and give it back to them. If the horse gets a little upset at this stage, it is better that you can hand it back to your assistant rather than dropping it because this action could in itself upset the horse. In an emergency, however, it is better to drop it than hang on to it and cause further problems.

It is a simple case of initially building up your horse's confidence so that he will accept the *garrocha* without question, even if mistakes do happen later when you might bounce it on his quarters or catch his ears or head with it. By the time you are trying more complicated movements your horse will be confident and you more competent.

To be a true artist with a *garrocha*, riding must become as second nature. Each and every complex movement and turn on a horse at the gallop or canter can be difficult enough with two hands, when all you have to focus on is the movement itself. By placing a *garrocha* in the right hand the difficulty factor rises; add to this an arena with an audience and dimmed lights, and the possibilities for error are endless: dropping the *garrocha*, the horse standing on his hind legs as you try to pirouette under the *garrocha*, banging your horse's head (which does nothing for the horse/rider relationship) and nearly taking a spectator's eye out with the pointy end, which does nothing to endear you to the crowd or enhance the performance!

Describing incidents like these may seem amusing but if they really happen, nobody will be laughing. It is simply my way of emphasizing that handling the *garrocha* must not be taken lightly. It is essential to practise the movements with and without the *garrocha*; riding many circles at walk, keeping the point in one place at the ground and your right hand over the pommel, will tell just how accurate your circles are. You must practise until every circle is the same and the right hand does not move.

For me, presenting the work with the *garrocha* as an art, as theatre, is what drives me to continuously pursue the correctness in the work. It is not always as you would wish in the arena on the night, but by honestly monitoring your own and your horse's performance you can constantly correct and improve it for the delight of the audiences who give so much support, energy and emotion to a performance.

The Cross-over

I have said that today some of the finest *vaquera* riders have a classical background, such as the Jerez school, and Manuel Rodriguez Gonzalez (*Doma Vaquera* champion of Spain 2001 and *Doma de Trabajo* [Working Equitation] Gold Medallist 2000) is a good example of this. I was very privileged to be invited to watch Manuel ride at his home. I spent several days with his lovely family, all of whom rode exceptionally well and worked so hard together on the horses. Manuel's father was a *vaquera* judge who sent Manuel and his brothers to the Royal Andalusian School of Equestrian Art in Jerez.

When I went to watch Manuel, he started his demonstration on a Lusitano *clasica* horse, warming up with basic exercises, and then taking the horse through piaffe pirouettes, passage half-passes, Spanish walk and finally a levade; a depiction of truly classical work.

Manuel then rode his *vaquera* mare in a double bridle and with a continental dressage saddle. His schooling followed the same good principles as those of the *clasica* horse, using lateral work progressively to soften and call the horse to attention. He performed changes, pirouettes and trot passes that many a Grand Prix rider would be glad to do, and took the horse through the *medias vueltas* and *vueltas*.

Manolo is such a good example of a cross-over rider, and his understanding of both the *vaquera* and *clasica* styles is awe-inspiring; but it also demonstrates that, when ridden at this level, *vaquera* is exciting, demanding and extremely skilful.

Doma Clasica

Once you start discussing classical dressage with serious dressage riders it is easy to get lost in the debate of what exactly *is* classical dressage. On the one hand you have many dressage trainers and riders who say that what they do in competition dressage is classical, but in competition warm-up arenas you often see demonstrations of something that is definitely not classical.

In Spain the term *doma clasica* is used to describe both dressage up to the level of high-school work and competition dressage under FEI rules, which can be confusing in itself, but it does differentiate them from *doma vaquera*, the stockman's dressage.

Classical dressage as seen in the Spanish Riding School of Vienna, the Portuguese School of Equestrian Art and the Royal Andalusian School of Equestrian Art is the true equestrian art form, full of grace, beauty and exquisite artistic expression. It is not a competition, there are no prizes, and herein lies the major difference. In each of these schools the emphasis is on working together, not as individuals, to achieve a particular goal, which might explain why, in days gone past, the original schools were considered to be not only academies of horsemanship but were also thought of as finishing schools for gentlemen.

In these schools today you will witness co-operation and co-ordination between not only man and horse but multiples of men and horses. In the work in-hand, two, or occasionally three, men must work together to teach the airs above the ground. They do this with little verbal communication. They have each learnt what is required and must trust each other to perform their part of a complicated and sometimes explosive manoeuvre.

A further example of this co-operation is seen in a quadrille of twelve horses, where the art is in the synchronization of twenty-four minds and bodies. As each and every individual step of the dance is taken, there must be a constant balance between the natural gaits of all the horses. Where some may find it easier to go faster in the trot they must be maintained at a speed such as the slowest or smallest-striding horse can keep up without recognizable effort. Whilst all the horses must be at the same level of training to be able to perform every movement within the piece, the achievement is judged by the successful co-ordination of the whole. This is a difficult task for all concerned, especially the leader, whose timing must be impeccable to set the pace throughout and bring the group to halt as the musician plays the final note.

When you are watching a quadrille, it is not the expressive change, or the tracking-up in the trot, or the amount of cross-over of the legs in the passes that is important, or even noticed, but the sheer beauty of so much harmony in movement; the describing of perfect patterns in the sand, and the amazing co-operation of so many stallions; and for some, being a part of this is far more exhilarating or satisfying than winning alone.

In the classical school it is not those horses who could be Grand Prix superstars who are required for the quadrille – or indeed many of the other aspects of the work – the requirements are quite different. The ultimate quality required is the control of any urge to kick or bite another stallion with whom they are in such close proximity, and astute selection, good training and working the stallions together virtually eliminates this. But it is a tribute to the Andalusians, Lusitanos and Lipizzaners that this can be done with such spirited stallions, and so well. Bringing twelve equine minds and bodies (and their riders')into alignment is a far harder task than that of the competition dressage rider, who only has the single horse/rider partnership to bring to ultimate readiness for competition.

The emphasis in quadrilles, then, is on the co-ordination of the routines; the beauty of the overall picture of the group and not the individual. Whilst we may watch individuals for a moment, we do not concentrate on them, but again and again go back to the intricate patterns and shapes that are presented to us. To maintain this flowing picture, all the riders must use their peripheral vision in order to be constantly aware of their positioning; to keep an equal distance between themselves and the horses to the front and sides of them. This alone may require minor adjustments at any moment to sustain the impression that all the horses are joined together by an invisible thread, which is quite the opposite of the ideal of absolute regularity within the gait for the competition horse.

The same principle of the whole being more important than the individual also applies to the *paso a dos* (pas de deux) or the *paso a tres* (pas de trois). Whilst it is easier to work two or three horses together than twelve, it is more important that a smaller number of horses are very similar, and finding two or three horses of the same size, who look the same and move the same, is no simple task. Also, although the more difficult movements and manoeuvres are easier to co-ordinate with a lesser number of horses, getting them trained to the same high level with enough movements within their repertoire to hold an audience spellbound for five minutes or more only compounds the difficulty. Finally, when two or three horses have worked so intensely together they have to be fit and sound on the day of the performance, because it will be hard to find a last-minute stand-in if a horse becomes lame or sick.

The classical solo is the nearest thing to the individual performance of the competition dressage rider, but there the comparison ends. In the dressage competition's freestyle to music, the competitor will work, sometimes for years, perfecting a test to music which has been very carefully put together to fit a particular horse's best rhythms and movements. Each section of the test has a different piece of music that is planned to enhance it. Unfortunately, at its worst, poorly selected music, such as some of the Eurovision-style songs or perhaps the popular classics with drum backing and computerized rhythm section (often made worse by poor cutting and sound quality), make even a well-ridden test seem less than adequate. When the music is tastefully selected and professionally edited, however, world-class performances, with their military-precision timing and near-perfect movements, can be fantastic.

These top-class performances notwithstanding, in competition the idea is to attain the maximum points for all aspects of the test by capitalizing on the horse's best features, whether it be outstanding extension, an astonishing piaffe or passage tour, or perhaps a double pirouette in perfect rhythm, and making a not-so-good natural walk, or any other poor characteristic, less obvious. Obviously, the ultimate aim is to ride a near-perfect test but, to achieve this, the rider must concentrate on precision to such a degree that, even at higher levels of competition, it can lead to dull, routinely performed tests and automated, bored horses. Some of these competition riders are obviously talented and skilled, and work hard to achieve the accolades they receive, but others ride in a way that is obviously hard work and harsh. This can sometimes be an unfortunate consequence of the competitive instinct.

By comparison, performances in the classical school are distinguished by their softness and ease that makes them so aesthetically pleasing. Away from the pressure of competition there is the opportunity to create an artistic interpretation of another kind, one where the footfall of the horse does not always have to coincide with the beat of the music, and the music is not edited a dozen times in five minutes. Here, the emphasis can be on the interpretation of the music and the artistry of the overall impression; the accuracy of the positioning of the change of movement or direction can give way to the beauty of the movement itself allowing, for example, a particularly elevated and harmonious piaffe or passage to reach a crescendo with a particular moment in a symphony that plucks the strings of the emotions of all who see it. Surely a moment like this is every bit a portrayal of pure art as the Mona Lisa.

Truly classical riders will remain so, even in the white heat of top-level competition. Juan Antonio Jimenez Cobo riding Enrique Guerro's Guizo at the 2004 Olympic Games.

Perhaps this artistic impression is the one way in which we can differentiate between competition and classical performances. To underline this, performances by the classical schools are often seen in wonderful settings and buildings of true architectural value, which when lit with an artist's eye do so much to add to the canvas on which the equestrian picture is painted.

Further examples of classical equitation in competition – Carol McArdle on Victorioso, bred by the Guadiola stud, performing a canter pirouette (LEFT) and extended trot (BELOW) at the USDF's 'Champagne Classic' competition.

Competition Dressage

In former eras, stable workers on the large estates, or even in the smaller private households, were reliant on the goodwill of their masters for their livelihood and home, and would therefore not have had much to say about the long, arduous hours they had to spend strapping, handling, training, working and caring for horses for very little pay. The upside of this for the landowners was that they could produce good horses for a very low cost.

Bearing this in mind you can see why nowadays, with all costs so much higher, taking the time to turn out well-produced horses is often commercially very difficult. So many horses are rushed through their training when a little more time spent on them would pay dividends. What is even more damaging is that well-bred horses are pushed too hard within the short span of their training, by trainers temperamentally unsuited to the task, which puts a lot of horses into the market-place who have been subjected to a daily routine of pressure and stress to a point that makes them far from suitable for the unsuspecting amateur. As a consequence, the fall-out rate for these poor horses is astounding.

There seems to be a desire to produce 'advanced' work and movements long before horses are mentally or physically ready, and then when they are unable to give what is required, they must suffer the retribution of these disappointed, inexperienced or mediocre trainers.

For those wishing to climb the competitive dressage ladder, there are more opportunities today to get good advice and help than there ever was. Many dressage conventions are held by world-class trainers such as Jo Hinnemann, Erik Tilgaard, Arthur Kottas, Conrad Schumacher and any number of others, who not only offer good, sound advice but are willing to show you how much of this work is done, openly and in a way that is within everyone's comprehension. We should be thankful that they are so prepared to help; I certainly have benefited greatly from their advice.

There are also more books, articles and videos than you would ever have time to study if you lived to be 150 years old, and clubs, groups and associations in abundance for those discerning riders who wish to seek good guidance in this fascinating pursuit called dressage.

Yet one thing I am always being told is, 'There are no trainers in my area', whatever that area is. If that is true, your time and money should be used wisely to search out a trainer who is best for you and your horse. There are still good, knowledgeable people out there who will help, and money is not always the answer. Even today, some trainers may be glad of some help for those times – some weekends, Christmas and holidays – for which it is difficult to get cover, in return for lessons. A dedicated, willing and reliable person should be able to come to some sensible and mutually agreeable arrangement with a trainer who can help them.

Those of you who wish to compete in dressage, whether at grass roots or international level, will do well to remember that winning is good, but not at any cost. It is not just you who is being pushed to win and, no matter how willing your horse may be, he has very little say in all the decisions you make to get there. You are not going to win without the right partner, so choose him wisely and take care of him along the way.

A systematic approach to your training is imperative. Initially you must try to find a horse with three good gaits – which is harder than you would imagine.

In the early stages, observing your horse at liberty or when you lunge him gives you the opportunity to see how he moves and whether he will truly take you as far as you wish to go. If your aim is modest and you are happy to stay at Preliminary and Novice levels (or your national equivalents), then the ability of the horse is not as important as that required for Grand Prix, at which level the precision of the work is tantamount to success.

We all have problems, disappointments and moments when things just don't work. On completion of a dressage test, most people can also acknowledge whether or not the judge has been fair or over-critical, because we should know our horses and our shortcomings. On the other hand a great many people can pull the wool over their own eyes as well as those of others in order to appear knowledgeable. Unfortunately, classical riding is one of those pursuits that to some is mystical and full of hidden secrets, making it easy for new-age 'masters of the art' to become the gurus of the time, and they are so surprised when they and their work are criticized by those who really know what to look for. It is imperative that we know what it is we are looking for in ourselves and our horses and check constantly that we are progressing in the right direction. For this we must be prepared to be critical of our work and our results. We should follow those who are truly knowledgeable and whose teachings are in line with what is proven, and be able to accept constructive criticism and good advice from them.

One way to do this is to compete, and here is where I talk about something I have not done, so I can be fairly criticized for not having had the experience of being before judges in a competition and I do accept this. However, if the proof of the pudding is in the eating, I have, in a way, been in front of judges on numerous occasions, having performed solo and with my friends more than a thousand times since 1988. In this sense, I feel that I have been judged by hundreds of thousands of spectators whenever I have performed, and many of these people are extremely knowledgeable.

One such time was at Hickstead, at the CDIO Championships. Having performed each day in the main arena, with some eight horses in the team, I was invited to perform a *garrocha* display in front of some of the best dressage riders and showjumpers in the world, just before we all went to dinner. This was a great honour, if not a little nerve-racking.

I have had no less than three List 1 judges in my yard: the Countess of Inchcape, Delia Cunningham and Jane Kidd. They spent a whole afternoon watching Danielle and me train, and I learnt a great deal from them all. A number of serious and knowledgeable competitors with enthusiasm for the Iberian horse have also come to watch us work, and some were very willing to explore different views and ideas.

I watch competitions, got to clinics and have had the pleasure to watch and work with some superb riders and trainers. The pleasure and knowledge gained when conversing over dinner with these people is immeasurable.

Whilst on the subject of dressage judges, let us spare a thought for them. They get a lot of criticism from competitors and onlookers alike and certainly some of it is warranted; there are unfair, unsympathetic and biased judges, but there are those who are knowledgeable, dedicate their life to the sport and put so much back into it by judging. They travel immense distances, sit in cold cars, are treated rudely by those who do not do well, and are sometimes not looked after by the organizers. A little understanding and appreciation from all sides helps everyone to benefit from participating in dressage competitions.

Those of you embarking on competitive dressage for the first time with your Spanish or Lusitano horse will see that, at the lower levels, the judging may vary dramatically for horses who do not fall into the category of Warmblood, the type that still dominates the dressage scene today. This is because less experienced judges, in particular, are sometimes diverted from their key task of assessing qualities such as freedom and regularity of movement, impulsion and submission, looking instead at the overall *type* of movement which they believe to be in vogue, and which may be represented chiefly by some particular breed or type.

This has, in fact, been an issue that has long pervaded the competition dressage scene: some years ago the Hanoverian was dominant and years before that the Thoroughbred crosses and Anglo-Arabs were popular. But there have always been exceptions that shone through: for example, the famous

Thoroughbred Wily Trout, ridden by the brilliant Christopher Bartle, did very well during the 'Hanoverian years' and some Arabs have shown a resurgence, going to Grand Prix level in recent years.

The situation presently is that the Northern Europeans have bred a type of horse that is strong, has big movement, is generally steady temperamentally and is, in many cases, suitable for a wide range of riders. These big horses fill the arena with their big trots and, in particular their tremendous extensions (something today's judges like to see). They can be trained and ridden in a strong and heavy style that a hot-blooded horse just would not tolerate – that is not to say that all Warmblood horses are, or indeed need to be, ridden like that, but it does appear to be a trait of modern competition dressage that has its supporters (and its critics).

The Spanish and Lusitano horses are a different matter altogether: many competition riders have been known to ride them but got off very quickly when they realized that the Iberians are just too fine for them. It is a talented and tactful rider who can ride both a Warmblood and a horse of this type.

No other horse has taken the modern dressage world by storm in such a surprising way, however, as has the Spanish Pure-bred. In the last decade Ignacio Ramblas and Evento changed everything for the Spanish horse in competition dressage. They performed with such *joie de vivre*, such *brio* (spirit) and such pure beauty in motion that there could be no doubt that the classical master, the horse of kings, was back where he belonged: ruling the manège.

They have brought not only grace but excitement to what is considered by many spectators to be a dull sport. Only the Spanish dare leave the arena at Spanish walk after a performance, arousing such a roar from the crowd. Since the Atlanta Olympics, the Spanish have done consistently well with their Pura Raza Españolas. Rafael Soto and Invasor – a horse who would not have looked out of place in the baroque period – simply stun every audience with their piaffes, passages and pirouettes. Whilst Invasor struggles to compete with the Warmbloods in the extended work, his collected work is superb.

Of all the nationalities that compete in dressage at international level today, the Spaniards, with their Spanish Pure-breds have, perhaps ironically, become the new arrivals.

The Principle of Competition Dressage

Competition dressage is a medium by which, in principle you can judge whether or not your training has reached a particular level and if the work is correct. As a rider wishing to improve you can, by systematically training yourself and your horse to each successive, more advanced, level, competing at this level and getting feedback from the judges, go as far as possible without missing out vital chunks of training.

Those people who choose to stay at unaffiliated lower levels indefinitely, knowing that they are good at these levels and will, more than likely, be in line for a prize, are quite obviously doing their horses a grave injustice. I know

RIGHT AND OPPOSITE

Juan Antonio Jimenez Cobo and Guizo – one of the combinations spearheading the resurgence of Spanish horses in international dressage.

some associations have awards for the most points earned in any one year in any form of competition, whether it be dressage, jumping, showing and so on. Whilst it is commendable that people try to earn the hundreds or even thousands of points they do, I feel that the principles behind it are somewhat lacking when you discover that almost all the points are won at the same level. It says to me that the participant has little interest in improving and more interest in trophies, however trivial they may be. Whatever level you are at, improvement must be possible.

Chapter Ten

Training the Rider

L EARNING IS NOT EASY. Where do I go? From whom do I learn? Who is right? We are all in this predicament at some time or other and often we find out the hard way, from a bad experience, who is just not right: the teacher who shouts, deliberately making us feel insecure or useless, or the teacher who is really only two steps ahead of us, if that!

Beware of False Gods

This section was one that just had to be written. Please do not feel that I am berating other trainers out of some petty jealousy or arrogance, but I do have an issue with some of the self-promotion, particularly under the 'alternative' or even classical banner, that implies their methods are new or unique.

There are many trainers who start off with the best of intentions before the commercial hype takes over, but there is an ever-increasing number of 'new experts' who have perhaps bought a schoolmaster who piaffes and passages a little and proceeded to parade the horse through as many promotional events as possible until they really believe that they are trainers and teachers of the 'Nouveau Moderne Classical School'. Unfortunately, the horse is probably ruined by this stage and the trainer's real experience is on the same level as their self-honesty.

The internet is a wonderful source of knowledge if you already have enough knowledge to distinguish between the truth and nonsense. It is very easy to set up a website and pontificate on the finer details of the most technical topic and in most cases most of us would not have a clue as to whether it was written by a genuine expert or someone who has merely gleaned the information directly from another site. In the equestrian world, such writing can be produced by someone with no real understanding of how a horse is actually ridden.

Imagine how you would feel if, after your first year of school dance classes, your teacher demanded that you learn the lead part in *Swan Lake* by a week next Saturday. And the teacher couldn't help you if she had never stepped on a stage or been on pointes in her life, even if she had seen the ballet and read the book.

The following are typical examples of what I call false gods.

You would be surprised at how many people enter the manège every day without a plan and proceed to wander all over the place like a mad woman possessed. This means that they have neither a plan for any given day, nor a systematic approach to the progression of training all together, often preferring to try things out at random as they think of them.

The following is a typical example of this random and directionless training. A rider came to me, having been introduced to me by a mutual friend, wanting help with piaffe and passage. I asked him to ride as if training at home so that I could get some idea of his understanding of training and execution of the movements.

First, he walked the horse in-hand in one direction only, holding his head to the inside in an attempt to do a shoulder-in. Three minutes later the horse was mounted and moved around from one spot to another in the arena, doing a variety of badly executed movements at walk then trot and, quite soon, canter. The rider finished off with a poor rendition of piaffe, which was like a soft-shoe shuffle with no co-ordination between front and back whatsoever, and a passage that was nothing more than the horse jolting forward because the rider slapped him with a stick. The rider then asked me what I thought.

My reply was as tactful as I could make it. I asked him how he thought he would fare in a dressage competition; he said that he didn't do dressage, and I could see why. I pointed out politely that, unfortunately, there was not one single movement or moment I could say was correct or in any way classical. The horse was unfit, slow, even lazy, permanently above the bit and hollow, did not track-up in walk or trot, and his lateral work was done with a crooked body and twisted head, a consequence mainly of the pull on the inside rein and absolutely no understanding of the outside rein.

I said that he should go right back to the beginning and learn what the criteria for each and every movement were, right from the very basics of movement within the gaits, and then build on that before he ruined another horse. These were harsh words, I know, but honesty, integrity and reality seemed to be lacking. In fact, this person went on to write a book on equitation.

Another example of self-promotion beyond self-knowledge was contained in an article on 'classical riding', which carried a picture of a horse who was quite obviously resisting and being naughty. The photograph was captioned: 'A young Lipizzaner offering a presentable levade in a playful moment.' Classical principles are not being portrayed if a young horse, quite obviously napping, is said to be performing a 'presentable levade'. There is a time to teach a levade and a method by which to teach it; the time is when the horse is more mature and educated, and the method is from collection. Neither of these principles was demonstrated by the picture, the caption or by any of the accompanying copy.

The point I am trying to make by giving these two rather raw examples is that it is unfair, misleading and confusing to readers who trust that what they read in a book or magazine (or observe at a demonstration or lesson) is correct, just because they are told it is.

We all make mistakes, but problems arise when people don't know what is right and what is wrong and, if it is wrong, how to correct it. When I look at a video or photos of my performance I know whether movements are correct or not, and when they are not I go back to the drawing board. If you know the criteria for a movement you will know when something is wrong; it follows, therefore, that anyone knowing the criteria for a levade would have known that the movement portrayed in that picture was wrong.

I have no wish to labour the point further, but the world is rapidly becoming full of instant celebrities and, in the horse world, every time someone acquires a previously well-trained horse, we get a new guru.

Finding the Right Teacher

I always advise people to take the time to find the right teacher: someone who has proved their ability, and who is prepared to let you watch them working and giving a lesson; even if there is a fee for their time it is surely worth a small investment rather than blindly going to any teacher and wasting a lot more money. Most importantly, it should be someone you can get on with in the long term, and someone who can teach you what you need to learn. Flitting from one trainer to another, covering the same ground until you find one that says you are excellent and your horse is perfect is pointless if you want to advance.

As with trainers of horses, there will always be those teachers who are self-elected experts. In addition to the 'false gods', who tend to be most evident in the 'noveau classical' world, there is an abundance of 'experts' in the horse world who will use any jargon-based, gimmick-propelled, commercialized claptrap to squeeze yet more of your hard-earned money out of you for a 'quick fix', or perhaps do anything rather than actually get out there and ride your horse, should the need arise. Of course, there are also some very talented people out there, who can teach a great deal, from a variety of angles – although I feel that every rider (and horse's) potential can best be realized by basing their training on the classical system and adding a good deal of common sense.

Ultimately, all teachers should be judged by their ability to pass on their knowledge, and by the development and abilities of their pupils. As a teacher myself, I am proud to be judged by the success of our display team and my many pupils, both in the UK and the USA, from the very novice to those at Grand Prix level.

Having a healthy, inquisitive mind and a willingness to at least consider other views, however hard that may be, is the foundation for expanding your knowledge. I freely admit to having been guilty of falling short in this regard on more than one occasion, something that I hope has been remedied with the help of a dear friend, Jules, who has been able to show me another point of view! However, it is a *discerning* mind that prevents you from wasting time and risking the mental and physical well-being of both you and your horse. Choose your mentors wisely.

In the following two sections, I will discuss a couple of issues that you should bear in mind when evaluating lessons either taken or observed.

The Lesson of the Day

It is good that teachers should be constantly open-minded and ready to absorb more and new information all the time and from whatever source. I have, however, come across many teachers who try to give 'the lesson of the day', something they have just read or seen (or have themselves just learnt from their trainer), regardless of its relevance to their pupil. Passing this straight on to every pupil and horse they meet will, on the whole, produce negative results; the information would be better filed away and brought out as and when it is appropriate. This is because every pupil/horse partnership is likely to be at a different level, or differ in their talents and/or problems, and so will require a technique or exercise structured specifically for them.

Whilst the fundamental principles are constant, assessment of each situation should result in an approach applicable to that partnership on that day, or indeed in that moment. Students are looking for guidance and the benefit of the teacher's experience, so that during each lesson they work on and assimilate something that is relevant to them; they do not just want to go over the same lesson, droned out parrot-fashion because 'That's what it says in the manual.'

The Art of Conversation and Simple Language

In building our repertoire of verbal and physical aids, we furnish ourselves with the language with which to converse with our horses whilst training and working. The language we hear or use in our everyday life can be simple or complicated. When we talk to our young children we use just a few small words and enunciate them clearly, but when we have to deal with the legal profession or discuss something particularly technical, the language used can be very bewildering. Some teachers use the language of equestrianism to bewilder, baffle and impress pupils in the same way as the worst kind of lawyer or scientist and, more often than not, this is done to cover up a lack of true knowledge and technical ability. Conversely, a good teacher will find the simplest, clearest and most appropriate way to put a point over to a particular pupil. Such a person will appreciate that the use of the appropriate language at the right time can make all the difference between being understood, misunderstood or ignored.

Note, on the other hand, that many talented *riders* (not *teachers*) are not good at articulating their methods and thoughts but work intuitively, instinctively and with passion. You will learn more from these people by observing them very closely indeed than by seeking to have actual lessons from them.

Learning by Observation

Take every opportunity to watch and listen to the very best; those who are truly at the top of their field, the chief riders at the Spanish Riding School of Vienna, or the chef d'equipe of a nation's dressage team, for example. Today, someone of this standing is Arthur Kottas; tomorrow it could be you.

Study the experts carefully: note their position, movement, balance, where they place their legs and hands, at what moment, and how, they ask for any movement. You may not understand as yet why and how all these things work, but these images will give you something to emulate and offer very definite benchmarks by which to compare your ability and that of your teachers. It is, of course, unrealistic to expect all teachers to be of this level, and there is a great need for good, honest teachers at all levels. However, having seen the best, you then have to find the teacher most likely to be able to help you on the path you have chosen.

Position, Position, Position

Instruction from a good teacher will always encompass the fact that your position in the saddle is of paramount importance. It will also acknowledge that, whilst the correct seat is an effective and elegant seat, a fixed, unforgiving and inconsiderate seat is arrogant and hard. The rider who sits like a centaur, upright and unmoving, may impress the uninformed spectator, but the true horseman is the rider whose seat lifts gently when the horse is struggling in piaffe, allowing the horse enough freedom to regain his energy and give brilliance to a movement that would had died. Your 'impressive' seat can stifle your horse's energy and ability, and can only reduce the potential for success. Furthermore, an overwhelming personality can do this to a horse whether in or out of the saddle.

A Long, Hard Road…but Enjoy the Journey

Riding well is about dedication and tenacity. You cannot do it unless you are 'doing it'. You have to be committed and be prepared to invest all you have into it. Like any great sportsman, artist or musician, you must have this dedication and commitment if you really want to achieve something. This does not mean that your goals have to be competitions and prizes, but simply to ride the best you can every time you get on a horse, to progress, and to finally feel at one with your horse.

Riding whilst drained or injured is what dedicated riders are known for, but 'this is just the physical pain', as my doctor friend Jeff once said when he fractured his wrist whilst in Portugal. Preferring to get it fixed in England he bandaged it and left it, saying: 'It's only carpentry; I'll sort it when I get home.' Riding is also about the mental pain: the criticism, both constructive and otherwise, the possible financial hardships and the feeling that, no matter how hard you try, you do not seem to make progress.

Relationships of all kinds can be pushed to the limit when put under pressure, especially if you focus solely on a particular element. Whether it is teacher and pupil, horse and rider, husband and wife, boyfriend and girlfriend or family and friends, any combination can be supportive or destructive when the desire for learning and success becomes intense. Falling out over the most ridiculous thing can bring about the end of a relationship. Therefore, give all you can to your pursuit but be considerate, understanding and fair, and always be prepared to say 'I am sorry', immediately, not three weeks later. A friendship is worth more than an opinion. Also, if you think about it, this attitude is equally important for your relationship with your horse.

Riding out the storm of negative aspects and never giving up will bring the reward of fulfilling your dreams, if that is what you really want in life. There will be times when you might want to give up; we all go through days when everything seems to go wrong, for whatever reason. You must also remember that when you are on form, your horse might be off form and vice versa, but as long as you understand yourself and your horse, you will be able to continue on the journey.

So, learning to ride well is not something that is achieved in a weekend, and you must be prepared to embark on a long journey, but a long journey that will be filled with enlightenment, understanding and wisdom: from the physical pleasure of working as one with your equestrian partner, to the mental stimulus and satisfaction of resolving a problem that has eluded and frustrated both you and your horse. It will enrich your life and add value to your existence. Any time spent in the company of the ones you love will never be wasted.

Recommended Reading

ISBNs are given for titles published since the introduction of that system.

Bennet, Deb, Ph.D., *Conquerors*, Amigo Publications, Inc. (USA) 1998, ISBN 0 9658533 0 6.

Burger, Üdo, *The Way to Perfect Horsemanship* (tr. Nicole Bartle), J.A. Allen (London) 1998, ISBN 0 85131 724 3. (First published as *Vollendete Reitkunst*, Paul Parey, Berlin and Hamburg 1959.)

Cunninghame Graham, R.B., *The Horses of the Conquest*, William Heinemann Ltd, (London) 1930.

Decarpentry, General Albert, *Academic Equitation* (tr. Nicole Bartle), J.A. Allen (London) 1987, ISBN 0 85131 821 5. (First published in France 1949.)

De la Guérinière, François Robichon, *School of Horsemanship* (tr. Tracy Boucher), J.A. Allen (London) 1994, ISBN 0 85131 575 5 (First published in a single volume as *Ecole de Cavalerie*, Paris 1733.)

Denhardt, Robert Moorman, *The Horse of the Americas*, University of Oklahoma Press 1948.

Fillis, James, *Breaking and Riding*, J.A. Allen (London) 1986, ISBN 0 85131 044 3. (First English edn. 1902.)

Hillsdon, Penny, *Pathfinder Dressage*, J.A. Allen (London) 2000, ISBN 0 85131 745 6.

Llamas, Juan, *This is the Spanish Horse* (tr. Jane Rabagliati), J.A. Allen (London) 1989, ISBN 0 85131 668 9. (First published by Juan Llamas, Madrid 1989.)

Loch, Sylvia, *The Royal Horse of Europe*, J. A. Allen (London) 1986, ISBN 0 85131 422 8.

Oliveira, Nuno, *Reflections on Equestrian Art*, (tr. Phyllis Field), J.A. Allen (London) 1988, ISBN 0 85131 461 9. (First published as *Reflexions sur l'Art Equestre*, Crépin Leblond, France 1964.)

Podhajsky, Alois, *The Complete Training of Horse and Rider* (tr. Eva Podhajsky), The Sportsman's Press (London) 1997.

Stanier, Sylvia, *The Art of Long Reining*, J.A. Allen (London) 1995, ISBN 0 85131 574 7.

Tinker, Edward Larocque, *Centaurs of Many Lands*, University of Texas Press (Austin) (Distributed in Great Britain by J. A. Allen) 1964.
—— *The Horsemen of the Americas*, University of Texas Press (Austin) 1967, Library of Congress Catalogue Card No. 65-23165.

Index